Maurice A. Crouse
3 April 1998

1

UNION HOME
PRAYER BOOK

CENTRAL CONFERENCE OF AMERICAN RABBIS

THE UNION HOME PRAYERBOOK

CONTENTS

PRAYERS FOR NIGHT AND MORNING

PRAYERS IN TIME OF SICKNESS AND DEATH

Prayers
for
Family Worship

FAMILY CEREMONY FOR THE
CONSECRATION OF A NEW HOME

Standing before a table on which are placed lighted candles, a loaf of bread, table salt, a cup of wine, a Bible, and a M'zuzo, the head of the family reads the following service:

Our God and God of our fathers, grant that we may consecrate this new home of ours with humble and grateful hearts. By Thy will we live and toil; by Thy grace we prosper and rejoice. We labor in vain when we labor without Thee; we build on shifting sand when Thou are not our Rock. In Thy goodness Thou dost bless us and cause us to dwell in comfort and peace. We give thanks unto Thee for Thine unfailing love and ever-watchful care.

בָּרוּךְ אַתָּה יְהֹוָה אֱלֹהֵינוּ מֶלֶךְ הָעוֹלָם
שֶׁהֶחֱיָנוּ וְקִיְּמָנוּ וְהִגִּיעָנוּ לַזְּמַן הַזֶּה:

Bo-ruch a-to A-do-noy Elo-he-nu Me-lech Ho-o-lom she-he-ch'yo-nu v'kiy'mo-nu v'hi-gi-o-nu la-z'man ha-ze.

Praised be Thou, O Lord, our God, Ruler of the world, who hast granted us life, sustained us, and permitted us to celebrate this joyous occasion.

HYMN

"O Worship the King," *Union Hymnal* 60, p. 61

RESPONSIVE READING

O give thanks unto the Lord, for He is good;
>   For His mercy endureth forever.

Happy is everyone that revereth the Lord,
>   That walketh in His ways.

When thou eateth the labor of thy hands,
>   Happy shalt thou be, and it shall be well with
>   thee.

Except the Lord build the house,
>   They labor in vain that build it.

I will walk within my house in the integrity of my
>   heart,
>   I will set no base thing before mine eyes.

He that worketh deceit shall not dwell within my
>   house;
>   He that speaketh falsehood shall not be
>   established before mine eyes.

The wicked are overthrown, and are not;
>   But the house of the righteous shall stand.

From of old our homes have been the dwelling
place of the Jewish spirit. Within their walls our
fathers built altars of faith and love. There they
maintained the habit of daily devotion; there they
prepared a table for the stranger and the needy.
Grant, O God, that we, too, may hallow our home
with devout thoughts and kindly acts. Give us the
will, we pray Thee, to keep alive at our fireside
the glow of simple piety and generous hospitality.

The loaf is cut into pieces which are dipped in salt and distributed; then, the blessing is said.

בָּרוּךְ אַתָּה יְהֹוָה אֱלֹהֵינוּ מֶלֶךְ הָעוֹלָם
הַמּוֹצִיא לֶחֶם מִן־הָאָרֶץ:

Bo-ruch a-to A-do-noy Elo-he-nu Me-lech Ho-o-lom
ha-motsi le-chem min ho-orets.

Praised be Thou, O Lord, our God, Ruler of the world, who causest the earth to yield food for all.

(Lifting wine-cup)

Wine is the symbol of joy. "Wine rejoiceth the heart of man." He who ordains life has made all the things that give us happiness. He has also established the home as the source of our deepest joys. We pray Thee, O God, that in our home love may reign and simple pleasures abound. Preserve in us devotion to virtue and simplicity, and enable us to spend our days in contentment, happiness and peace.

בָּרוּךְ אַתָּה יְהֹוָה אֱלֹהֵינוּ מֶלֶךְ הָעוֹלָם
בּוֹרֵא פְּרִי הַגָּפֶן:

Bo-ruch a-to A-do-noy Elo-he-nu Me-lech Ho-o-lom
bo-re p'ri ha-go-fen.

Praised be Thou, O Lord, our God, Ruler of the world, who hast created the fruit of the vine.

(Holding Bible)

This is the Law by which Israel has ever lived. It teaches us that man doth not live by bread only, but by everything that proceedeth out of the mouth of the Lord doth man live. We thank Thee, O God, for this Book of the Law, which Thou hast placed in our keeping for the good of all mankind. May it ever be a lamp unto our feet, and a light unto our path. Give us understanding, that we keep Thy law and observe it with our whole heart. Implant in us a love of Torah, that we may treasure it more than gold and silver, and take great delight in the study of its teachings.

בָּרוּךְ אַתָּה יְהֹוָה אֱלֹהֵינוּ מֶלֶךְ הָעוֹלָם
אֲשֶׁר קִדְּשָׁנוּ בְּמִצְוֹתָיו וְצִוָּנוּ לַעֲסוֹק בְּדִבְרֵי תוֹרָה:

Bo-ruch a-to A-do-noy Elo-he-nu Me-lech Ho-o-lom a-sher kid'sho-nu b'mits-vo-sov v'tsi-vo-nu la'asok b'divre so-ro.

Praised be Thou, O Lord, our God, Ruler of the world, who hast sanctified us by Thy Commandments and ordained that we occupy ourselves with the words of the Law.

(If a M'zuzo is affixed, turn to the Book of Deuteronomy and read from the scriptural passages inscribed on the parchment within the M'zuzo case—Chapter VI, verse 4 through 9, and from Chapter XI, verses 13 through 21)

(Raising the M'zuzo)

This ancient symbol of the M'zuzo speaks, then, to us of the One God, of our need to love Him and to obey His Law. We affix the M'zuzo to the door-post of our home that it may ever remind us of our divine nature and of the sacred duties of life. We have God in our hearts when our home thus bears witness to His holy presence.

Thou, O God, art our guardian and protector. Into Thy hands we commit our lives and destiny. Whatever may befall us, we shall not fear nor be dismayed; for Thou art with us. In Thee we trust; from Thee comes our strength; with Thee alone is the power to save.

The M'zuzo is fastened to the door-post and the following blessing is recited:

בָּרוּךְ אַתָּה יְהֹוָה אֱלֹהֵינוּ מֶלֶךְ הָעוֹלָם
אֲשֶׁר קִדְּשָׁנוּ בְּמִצְוֹתָיו וְצִוָּנוּ לִקְבֹּעַ מְזוּזָה:

Bo-ruch a-to A-do-noy Elo-he-nu Me-lech Ho-o-lom a-sher kid'sho-nu b'mits-vo-sov v'tsi-vo-nu lik-bo-a m'zuzo.

Praised be Thou, O Lord, our God, Ruler of the world, who hast sanctified us by Thy Commandments and ordained that we affix the M'zuzo.

Anthem: AMERICA

GRACE BEFORE MEALS

O Loving Father, whose bounty sustains us, we ask Thy favor for all Thy children. Bless this house and us assembled around this table. Unite our hearts in family love and strengthen our will to serve Thee in truth.

$$\text{בָּרוּךְ אַתָּה יְהֹוָה אֱלֹהֵינוּ מֶלֶךְ הָעוֹלָם}$$
$$\text{הַמּוֹצִיא לֶחֶם מִן הָאָרֶץ:}$$

Praised be Thou, O Lord, our God, who bringest forth food from the earth.

GRACE AFTER MEALS

O Lord, Thou art our Shepherd, and we shall not want. Thou openest Thy hand and satisfiest the needs of every living being. We thank Thee for the gifts of Thy bounty which we have enjoyed at this table. Thy kindness endureth forever, and we put our trust in Thee.

While we enjoy Thy gifts, may we never forget the needy, nor allow those who want, to be forsaken. May our table be an altar of loving-kindness, and our home a temple in which Thy spirit of goodness dwells.

$$\text{בָּרוּךְ אַתָּה יְיָ, הַזָּן אֶת־הַכֹּל:}$$

Praised be Thou, O Lord, who in kindness sustainest the world. AMEN.

SABBATH EVE

KIDDUSH

קִדּוּשׁ

*The table is given a festive appearance. A wine cup
and a loaf of bread for the blessing are set before the
head of the household. The ceremony of ushering in the
Sabbath is begun by the kindling of the lights, during
which a blessing by the wife is silently asked upon the
home and the dear ones. The following may be used:*

May our home be consecrated, O God, by Thy
light. May it shine upon us all in blessing as the
light of love and truth, the light of peace and good-
will. Amen.

When all are seated, the head of the household says:

Come, let us welcome the Sabbath in joy and
peace!

Like a bride, radiant and joyous, comes the
Sabbath. She brings blessings to our hearts; work-
day thoughts and cares are put aside. The brightness of the Sabbath light shines forth to tell that
the divine spirit of love abides within our home. In
that light all our blessings are enriched, all our
griefs and trials are softened.

At this hour, God's messenger of peace comes
and turns the hearts of the parents to the children,

and the hearts of the children to the parents; strengthening the bonds of devotion to that pure and lofty ideal of the home found in Sacred Writ.

* * * * * *

(*The following verses from Chapter 31 of the Book of Proverbs may be added*):

Whoso findeth a virtuous woman, far above pearls is her value.

She looketh well to the ways of her household and eateth not the bread of idleness.

She giveth provision to her household, and a task to her maidens.

She spreadeth out her open palm to the poor, yea, her hand she stretcheth forth to the needy.

She openeth her mouth with wisdom, and the law of kindness is on her tongue.

Strength and dignity are her clothing, and she smileth at the coming of the last day.

Her children rise up and call her blessed, her husband also; and he praiseth her saying: Many daughters have done virtuously, but thou excellest them all.

False is grace and vain is beauty; but a woman that feareth the Lord, she alone shall be praised.

Give her of the fruit of her hands, and let her own works praise her in the gates.

The head of the household lifts the wine cup and says:

Let us praise God with this symbol of joy, and thank Him for the blessings of the past week, for life, health, and strength, for home, love, and friendship, for the discipline of our trials and temptations, for the happiness that has come to us out of our labors. Thou hast ennobled us, O God, by the blessings of work, and in love and kindness Thou hast sanctified us by the blessings of rest through the commandment: "Six days shalt thou labor and do all thy work, but the seventh day is the Sabbath hallowed unto the Lord, Thy God."

בָּרוּךְ אַתָּה יְהֹוָה אֱלֹהֵינוּ מֶלֶךְ הָעוֹלָם
בּוֹרֵא פְּרִי הַגָּפֶן:

Praised be Thou, O Lord our God, King of the universe, who hast created the fruit of the vine.

The wine cup is passed round the table and each in turn drinks from it.

The head of the household then breaks the bread and, dipping a piece of it in salt, pronounces the blessing:

בָּרוּךְ אַתָּה יְהֹוָה אֱלֹהֵינוּ מֶלֶךְ הָעוֹלָם
הַמּוֹצִיא לֶחֶם מִן־הָאָרֶץ:

Praised be Thou, O Lord our God, King of the universe, who causest the earth to yield food for all.

Each one at the table likewise partakes of bread and salt.

Then the parent, with hands upon the head of each child in turn, silently pronounces such a blessing as the heart may prompt, or uses the following formula:

May the God of our fathers bless you. May He who has guided us unto this day lead you to be an honor to our family. May He who has protected us from all evil make you a blessing to Israel and to all mankind. AMEN.

II. SABBATH EVE

The mother lights the candles and recites the following:

Thou art our Light, O Lord, and our Salvation. In Thy Name we kindle these Sabbath lights. May they bring into our household the beauty of truth and the radiance of love's understanding. On this Sabbath eve, and at all times, "Let there be light."

בָּרוּךְ אַתָּה יְיָ אֱלֹהֵינוּ מֶלֶךְ הָעוֹלָם

אֲשֶׁר קִדְּשָׁנוּ בְּמִצְוֹתָיו וְצִוָּנוּ לְהַדְלִיק נֵר שֶׁל־שַׁבָּת:

Bo-ruch a-to A-do-noy Elo-he-nu Me-lech Ho-o-lom a-sher kid'sho-nu b'mits-vo-sov v'tsi-vo-nu l'had-lik nayr shel shab-bos.

Praised be Thou, Lord our God, King of the Universe, who hast sanctified us with Thy commandments and commanded us to kindle the light of the Sabbath.

The father raises the wine cup and recites:

Wine is the symbol of joy. On Sabbaths and Festivals, in the ancient Temple and in all the homes of Israel, our fathers lifted up the cup of happiness and proclaimed the name of the Lord. At His command they rose above their sorrows and honored the holy day with heartfelt joy. On this day we ask of Thee, O God, to shield us from sickness and sorrow. Strengthen us with Thy help and gladden us with Thy blessing. In our hearts and in our home let this be a Sabbath of joy.

בָּרוּךְ אַתָּה יְהֹוָה אֱלֹהֵינוּ מֶלֶךְ הָעוֹלָם
בּוֹרֵא פְּרִי הַגָּפֶן:

Bo-ruch a-to A-do-noy Elo-he-nu Me-lech Ho-o-lom bo-re p'ri ha-go-fen.

Praised be Thou, Lord our God, King of the Universe, who hast created the fruit of the vine.

The wine cup is passed around for all to taste.

* * * * * *

A child before an unbroken loaf of bread recites:

Bread is the staff of Life. The wheat, the corn and all the food which grows from the earth are the sign of God's blessing and the fruit of human work. For the bounty of nature's harvest, which rewards the work of man, we utter our thanks to the Father Eternal.

בָּרוּךְ אַתָּה יְהוָֹה אֱלֹהֵינוּ מֶלֶךְ הָעוֹלָם
הַמּוֹצִיא לֶחֶם מִן הָאָרֶץ:

Bo-ruch a-to A-do-noy Elo-he-nu Me-lech Ho-o-lom ha-motsi le-chem min ho-orets.

Praised be Thou, Lord our God, King of the Universe, who bringest forth food from the earth.

The bread is broken and all take a morsel, the blessing being repeated by the other children.

FOR THE EVE OF THE HOLIDAYS

KIDDUSH

קִדּוּשׁ

The table is given a festive appearance. A wine cup and a loaf of bread (on Passover, unleavened bread), for the blessing are set before the head of the household. Lifting the cup of wine he says:

בָּרוּךְ אַתָּה יְהֹוָה אֱלֹהֵינוּ מֶלֶךְ הָעוֹלָם שֶׁהֶחֱיָנוּ וְקִיְּמָנוּ וְהִגִּיעָנוּ לַזְּמַן הַזֶּה:

Blessed art Thou, O Lord our God, King of the universe, who hast granted us life, sustained us and permitted us to celebrate this joyous festival.

Feast of Pesach

Let us praise God with this symbol of joy and thank Him for the blessings which this Feast of Pesach brings to us. Our hearts are stirred by memories of deliverance of our forefathers from Egypt. The unleavened bread reminds us of the hardships they endured to remain steadfast to the service of God. May their example teach us fortitude, and lead us through noble living to the service of the Eternal God.

(The Benedictions, page 21)

Feast of Shabuoth

Let us praise God with this symbol of joy and thank Him for the blessings which this Feast of Shabuoth brings to us. God in His loving-kindness blessed our fathers by entrusting them with the Ten Commandments. May we renew, on this festival, the promise then made by our sires: "All that the Lord hath spoken, we will do and heed."

(The Benedictions, page 21)

Feast of Succoth

Let us praise God with this symbol of joy and thank Him for the blessings which this Feast of Succoth brings to us. May God's Providence which cared for our fathers in their wanderings also protect us.

His bounteous hand satisfies all needs. May our kindness to others show our gratitude to Him whose kindness endureth forever.

(The Benedictions, page 21)

NEW YEAR

Let us praise God with this symbol of joy and thank Him for the blessings which this New Year's day brings to us. Happy are we that God has granted us another year of life; and may it be His will to inscribe us for the coming year in the Book of Life, Happiness, and Peace.

BENEDICTIONS

בָּרוּךְ אַתָּה יְהֹוָה אֱלֹהֵינוּ מֶלֶךְ הָעוֹלָם
בּוֹרֵא פְּרִי הַגָּפֶן:

Praised art Thou, O Lord our God, King of the universe, who hast created the fruit of the vine.

The wine cup is passed round the table and each in turn drinks from it.

The head of the household then breaks the bread (on Passover the unleavened bread) and, dipping it in salt, pronounces the blessing:

בָּרוּךְ אַתָּה יְהֹוָה אֱלֹהֵינוּ מֶלֶךְ הָעוֹלָם
הַמּוֹצִיא לֶחֶם מִן הָאָרֶץ:

Praised art Thou, O Lord our God, King of the universe, who causest the earth to yield food for all.

Each one at the table likewise partakes of the bread and salt.

Then the parent, with hands upon the head of each child in turn, silently pronounces such a blessing as the heart may prompt; or uses the following formula:

May the God of our fathers bless you! May He who has guided us unto this day lead you to be an honor to our family. May He who has protected us from all evil make you a blessing to Israel, and all mankind.   AMEN.

CELEBRATION OF HANUKKAH

Hanukkah, or Feast of Dedication, lasts eight days. On the first evening one light is kindled, the number of lights being increased by one on each successive evening. Before the kindling of the lights, the following is said:

Praised art Thou, O Lord our God, King of the universe, who wonderfully helped our fathers at this season in days of yore.

בָּרוּךְ אַתָּה יְהֹוָה אֱלֹהֵינוּ מֶלֶךְ הָעוֹלָם
שֶׁהֶחֱיָנוּ וְקִיְּמָנוּ וְהִגִּיעָנוּ לַזְּמַן הַזֶּה:

Praised art Thou, O Lord our God, King of the universe, who hast granted us life, sustained us and permitted us to celebrate this joyous festival.

After kindling the lights, say the following:

Praised art Thou, O Lord our God, King of the universe, for the inspiring truths of which we are reminded by these Hanukkah lights.

We kindle them to recall the great and wonderful deeds wrought through the zeal with which God filled the hearts of the heroic Maccabees. These lights remind us that we should ever look unto God whence comes our help.

As their brightness increases from night to night, let us more fervently give praise to God for the ever-present help He has been to our fathers in the gloomy nights of oppression and trouble.

The sages and heroes of all generations made every sacrifice to keep the light of God's truth burning brightly. May we and our children be inspired by their example; so that at last, Israel may be a guide to all men on the way of righteousness and peace.

PSALM CXXI

I lift up mine eyes unto the mountains: whence shall come my help?

My help is from the Lord, the Maker of heaven and earth.

He will not suffer thy foot to slip: thy keeper doth not slumber.

Behold, He slumbereth not, and He sleepeth not—the Guardian of Israel.

The Lord is thy keeper: the Lord is thy shade; He is on thy right hand.

By day the sun shall not strike thee, nor the moon by night.

The Lord will guard thee against all evil: He will guard thy soul.

The Lord will guard thy going out and thy coming in from this time forth and forever more.

II

HANUKKAH SERVICE FOR THE HOME

Each day the children take turns in reciting the blessing. This is followed by the reading of the daily paragraph for the Servant Light and the special paragraph for the day. After the lighting of the candles all present should join in singing the Hanukkah Hymn.

THE BLESSING (Hebrew or English) (EACH DAY)

Bo-ruch a-to A-do-noy Elo-he-nu Me-lech Ho-o-lom a-sher kid'sho-nu b'mits'-vo-sov v'tsi-vo-nu l'had-lik nayr shel chan-nu-kah.

Praised be Thou, Lord our God, King of the universe, who hast ennobled us by Thy commandments and commanded us to kindle the Hanukkah lights.

THE SERVANT LIGHT OR SHAMMASH (EACH DAY)

As one candle may kindle many others and yet lose none of its own light, so Judaism has kindled the light of truth for many religions in many lands and still shines brightly through the ages.

For the First Day:

The first light tells of Him whose first command was "Let there be light." The darkness of idol-worship was scattered when Israel brought the radiant knowledge of the One God. "I am the first and I am the last", saith the Lord.

For the Second Day:

The second is the light of the Torah. Israel's book of law has brought learning and truth to all the western world. "The commandment is a lamp and the Law is a light."

For the Third Day:

The third is the light of Justice. No nation can endure which is unjust to the weak. "Justice always Justice shalt thou pursue" was the grandest command of Moses, our teacher.

For the Fourth Day:

The fourth is the light of Mercy. Cruelty hardens the heart and destroys friendship. "Do justice and love mercy" was the teaching of Micah the prophet.

For the Fifth Day:

The fifth is the light of Holiness. Purity of thought, nobility of action make all of life sacred. From the prophet Isaiah these words have been taken into Israel's prayerbook—"Holy, holy, holy is the Lord of Hosts."

For the Sixth Day:

The sixth is the light of Love. When the love which our parents gives us makes all our life beautiful, we learn to understand the Biblical words, "Thou shalt love the Lord thy God with all thy heart and soul and might."

For the Seventh Day:

The seventh is the calm light of Patience. Nothing can be achieved in haste. The spreading trees and the soul of man grow slowly to perfection. Thus sang King David, "Trust in the Lord, wait patiently for Him."

For the Eighth Day:

The eighth is the light of Courage. Let truth and justice be your armor and fear not. Judas Maccabeus, the hero of Hanukkah, lived by the words which Moses spoke to Joshua: "Be strong and of good courage."

HANUKKAH SONG

(Music in the *Union Hymnal*, page 117)

Rock of Ages, let our song
    Praise Thy saving power;
Thou, amidst the raging foes,
    Wast our sheltering tower.
Furious they assailed us,
But Thine arm availed us;
      And Thy word
      Broke their sword
When our own strength failed us.

Kindling new the holy lamps,
    Priests approved in suffering,
Purified the nation's shrine,
    Brought to God their offering.
And His courts surrounding
Heard, in joy abounding,
      Happy throngs
      Singing songs
With a mighty sounding.

Children of the Martyr-race,
    Whether free or fettered,
Wake the echoes of the songs
    Where ye may be scattered!

Yours the message cheering,
That the time is nearing
　　Which will see
　　All men free,
Tyrants disappearing.

THANKSGIVING DAY

(Before the Meal)

O Lord of the Universe and Protector of all mankind, from Thee come all our blessings from day to day and from year to year. How great is Thy loving-kindness, O God. The sheltering mountains and the shaded forests, the abundant streams and the fruitful earth tell of Thy bountiful goodness.

In this land of ours so richly blessed by Thee, we raise our voice in joyous thanks. To these shores Thy children have come from many climes seeking liberty and a new hope in life. All have been pilgrims to this western world. Here they found renewed purpose, increased strength and the opportunity to outgrow old fears and suspicions. For America, for the freedom of its laws, the richness of its natural blessing and the growing comradeship of its citizens, we praise Thee, O God, in humble Thanksgiving. O, continue Thy loving-kindness to our beloved country. As Thou hast blessed it in the past, so renew Thy bounty in the years to come.

"America, America, God shed His grace on
    thee,
And crown thy good with brotherhood, from
    sea to shining sea."

בָּרוּךְ אַתָּה יְהֹוָה אֱלֹהֵינוּ מֶלֶךְ הָעוֹלָם
הַמּוֹצִיא לֶחֶם מִן הָאָרֶץ:

Praised be Thou, O Lord our God, King of the universe, who causest the earth to yield food for all.

BIRTHDAY CELEBRATION

O eternal God, Thou art the Master of our destiny and the source of all life. Our times are in Thy hand. We thank Thee day by day for Thy manifold blessings and, as year follows year, we are grateful that Thou hast sustained us.

We gather today in special joy and thankfulness to share in the happiness of our dear _____. It is Thou who hast granted him (her) strength and life. Bless him (her), O Lord, with health and joy. Sustain him (her) in times of sickness and console him (her) in days of sorrow. Endow him (her) with long life and abundance of blessing; and grant to us the joy of meeting, for many years, as on this day, a loving family in mutual reverence and unbroken unity.

בָּרוּךְ אַתָּה יְהֹוָה אֱלֹהֵינוּ מֶלֶךְ הָעוֹלָם
שֶׁהֶחֱיָנוּ וְקִיְּמָנוּ וְהִגִּיעָנוּ לַזְּמַן הַזֶּה:

Praised be Thou, O Lord, our God, who hast kept us in life, sustained us and brought us to this happy day.

בָּרוּךְ אַתָּה יְהֹוָה אֱלֹהֵינוּ מֶלֶךְ הָעוֹלָם
הַמּוֹצִיא לֶחֶם מִן־הָאָרֶץ:

Praised be Thou, O Lord our God, Ruler of the world, who causest the earth to yield food for all.

ANNIVERSARY OF THOSE RECENTLY MARRIED

O Thou who hast blessed our fathers of old, bestow Thy blessing upon _____. Cause them to prosper in the way of life which they shall pursue, sharing with one another life's trials as well as life's joys, and thereby finding grace in the eyes of all who see them. Aid them to build a home that shall honor the house of Israel. May peace ever dwell within their home; contentment, love and joy within their hearts. May they grow old together in health and be ever grateful unto Thee for their union. AMEN.

SILVER OR GOLDEN WEDDING ANNIVERSARY

Eternal God and Father! In the fullness of this day's joy, we turn our hearts in praise and gratitude to Thee. We thank Thee for Thy favor which has preserved and sustained this happy couple and permitted them to reach this hour. In the midst of family (and friends) and loved ones, they look back in reverent and grateful reminiscence upon the stretch of years since first they pledged their hearts to one another and to Thee. Many and varied have been the experiences since that hour; many have been the mingled occasions of victory and defeat, of fulfillment and disappointment. We thank Thee

for the joys unnumbered with which Thou hast
sweetened their lives; and likewise, we praise Thee
for the trials which, with Thy help, they have
surmounted. Our times are in Thy hand; we know
that Thou wilt guide and sustain us even unto the
end. As Thou hast blessed them in the past, so
continue to bless them in the years to come. May
it be Thy will that these be years of health and
contentment; of unclouded bliss in the circle of
their family and loved ones; of mutual and unbroken service of righteousness, love and peace to
those who are far and to those who are near.
AMEN.

*If a rabbi participates in the celebration, continue as
follows:*

Rabbis' Manual, page 46 line 5—Even as you—
to the bottom of page 47.

PRAYER IN THE HOUSE OF MOURNING

We are assembled with our friends in the shadow that has fallen on their home. We raise our voices together in prayer to the Father above, asking for comfort and strength. We need light when gloom darkens our home; whence can it come but from the Creator of light? We need fortitude and resignation under the chastening of the Lord; whence can these come save from Him who lays the burden upon us? Who among us has not passed through trials and bereavements! Some bear fresh wounds in their hearts and therefore feel the more keenly the kinship of sorrow. Others whose days of mourning are more remote, still recall the comfort that sympathy brought to their sorrowing hearts. And those of us who have not yet tasted of the bitter cup cannot know how soon we may be called on to drink of it. All that we prize is but lent to us and we must surrender it when God demands. We are travelers on the same road which leads to the same end.

Eternal is Thy power, O Lord, Thou art mighty to save. In loving-kindness Thou sustainest the living; in the multitude of Thy mercies, Thou preservest all. Thou upholdest the falling and healest the sick, freest the captives, and keepest faith with Thy children in death as in life. Who is like unto Thee, Almighty God, Author of life and death,

Source of salvation? Praised be Thou, O Lord, who hast implanted within us eternal life.

PSALM XXIII

The Lord is my shepherd; I shall not want,

He maketh me to lie down in green pastures;

He leadeth me beside the still waters.

He restoreth my soul;

He guideth me in straight paths for His name's sake.

Yea, though I walk through the valley of the shadow of death,

I will fear no evil,

For Thou art with me;

Thy rod and Thy staff, they comfort me.

Thou preparest a table before me in the presence of mine enemies;

Thou hast anointed my head with oil; my cup runneth over.

Surely goodness and mercy shall follow me all the days of my life;

And I shall dwell in the house of the Lord forever.

KADDISH (Page 91)

For complete service see Union Prayerbook, N. R. page 300.

DEDICATION OF A TOMBSTONE

All-kind and merciful Father, a thousand years in Thy sight are but as yesterday, and the years of our life are but as a span; yet dost Thou grant us the blessed comfort of prolonging on earth the loving memory of our dear ones.

In Thine unsearchable wisdom, Thou hast taken our dear _____ from us. But the deep and tender love which attached us to our _____, is as strong as death. Striving to soothe the sorrow of our hearts, we dedicate this stone today.

In consecrating it unto the memory of the departed, may we at the same time dedicate unto the living the love with which our dear one filled our lives. So may we realize the truth of Sacred Writ: "The memory of the righteous is a blessing."

In this spirit, O God, we offer our prayers to Thee. Fill our hearts with humility that we may truly know that Thy thoughts are not our thoughts. Help us to live that the purity and godliness of our lives may bring honor to the memory of the dear ones who dwell in peace with Thee. Thus shall we erect for them their truest, their everlasting memorial among men. May the soul of our departed be bound up in life everlasting. Praised be unto Thee, O God, who givest life and takest it away. AMEN.

In the name of the family of our late brother (sister) and in the presence of this assemblage of relatives and friends, we consecrate this monument to his (her) memory, as a token of respect and love.

May his soul be bound up in the bond of eternal life.

KADDISH (Page 91)

FAMILY YAHRZEIT LIGHT CEREMONIAL

The family is gathered at dusk, before the evening meal, on the eve of the anniversary of the death of the departed. The head of the family speaks:

Dear Ones—at this moment which bears the memory of our beloved _____, let us join hands in token of God's grace. A link has been broken in the chain of affection which has long bound us together, yet the blessed bonds of home and love remain. With prayerful hearts, we receive this divine gift of life which holds us together in family union.

Eternal God, we thank Thee that in the hour of bereavement Thou didst sustain us. Though sorrow lingers in our memory, we have learned that love is stronger than death. At Thy command, our loved one has gone to his (her) eternal rest. To Thee we lift grateful hearts, for we sense our beloved in our very midst as a living presence. We

acknowledge Thy mercy, O Father, who doth
strengthen Thy children with faith and peace.

*At this point it would be appropriate for members of
the group to recite a passage from the Bible or Prayerbook which was a favorite of the departed, or to recall
intimate characteristics and tender incidents in his or
her life.*

As our dear one lives again for us in these words
and memories, we kindle the Yahrzeit Light and
sanctify it in the remembrance of the Divine Word:
"The spirit of man is the candle of the Lord."

Kindle the light.

זֵכֶר צַדִּיק לִבְרָכָה: *Zecher tsadik liv'rocho.* The
memory of the righteous is a blessing.

KADDISH (Page 91)

Personal Prayers
for
Special Occasions

ON TAKING A JOURNEY

"The Lord shall guard thy going out and thy coming in from this time forth and forever."

Psalm 121, 7

Lord of the Universe, the whole world is full of Thy glory. Wherever I may journey, Thou art near me to shield and to guide. "If I take the wings of the morning and dwell in the uttermost part of the sea; even there would Thy hand lead me, and Thy right hand would hold me."

With grateful heart I thank Thee, O Lord, for all Thy guidance in the past. Thou hast been a light to my path. Thou hast shielded me on my journeying in the past and brought me safely back to my home. Now that I begin a new journey, I turn to Thee, O Lord, confident of Thy guidance. O guard Thou me against the perils of the road. Keep me in health and bring me safely to my destination. Grant that this journey be not in vain but that the purposes of my travel be fulfilled. Shield me on my return and bring me back in health to my dear ones. Bestow Thy blessing upon me as I depart and when, with Thy help, I shall return. AMEN.

PRAYER AFTER PASSING THROUGH DANGER

My times are in Thy hand, O God, and Thy tender mercies are ever near me.

Now that Thou hast delivered me, O God, from this unlooked for calamity, accept my most fervent words of prayer and thanks. According to my strength, help me to bring Thy comfort to all who suffer. Teach me to number my days, that I may apply my heart unto wisdom.

Help me to be calm in the presence of danger that I may bear all ordeals, trustful of Thy help.

Blessed art Thou, O Lord our God, King of the Universe, who art the guardian of all Thy children, who slumberest not and sleepest not.   AMEN.

BEGINNING A NEW ENTERPRISE

"Unless the Lord build the house, they labor in vain that build it."   *Psalm 127, 1*

O Creator of the Universe by whose will the world is renewed day by day, Thou hast implanted in us a spark of Thy creative spirit. Thou dost arouse us from lethargy and dost send us forth to work and to achieve. Thus are we impelled to seek improvement, to make new plans, to organize and to build. For this creative impulse, for the desire to progress, for the urge towards greater achievement, we thank Thee, O Creator. Thou hast made us partners of Thee in the building of the world.

Often we cannot tell whether what we build is in harmony with Thy larger plans. It may, alas, happen that our structures are morally ugly and mar the landscape of Thy creation. We need Thy guidance day by day. Therefore I pray to Thee:— Guard Thou my steps in the new enterprise which I am about to begin. Grant that its success be not built upon the ruins of another's failure; that no added prosperity which may come to me will increase the misery of my fellowman.

Thine earth is bountiful. Thou openest Thy hand and satisfiest all with Thy favor. May, therefore, the achievement which I hope to attain for myself and my dear ones add also to the contentment of others. Let my work be done in harmony with Thy laws of justice, goodness and truth.

Strengthen me, O Lord, in the enterprise which I am now beginning. Make clear to my vision that I may discern the outlines of the future. Make strong my will that I may not falter when the tasks grow heavy. Make wise my judgment that I be not led into folly. More than for all these blessings, I pray, O Lord, that the strains of new work shall not injure my health, nor so absorb my energies that I neglect my dear ones, or become estranged from the worship of Thee. Let me walk in the light of Thy presence so that success will add to my spiritual strength and my achievement be a source of encouragement and blessing.   AMEN.

PRAYER OF A BRIDEGROOM

Almighty God and Father, as I am about to enter into the bond of wedlock, I pray for Thy light and Thy blessing. Open my eyes to see that the love in my heart is a gift from Thy hand, to increase my happiness and to add worth and significance to my life. Help me to fulfil all the duties of my new life. May I always be worthy of the trust and devotion of my beloved. May I always be to her a faithful husband, a true friend and protector.

Let Thy blessing rest upon the home we shall establish together. May it be a home where love and peace, mutual forbearance and devotion shall always abide. May the spirit of religion ever pervade its atmosphere. Give me the vision to see that without Thy presence to sustain and comfort us we shall fail to fulfil the divine plan of our lives.

May ours be a union of hands for honest toil and fruitful effort. May we work and strive together through days of joy and sorrow, to achieve the happiness for which our hearts are yearning.

PRAYER OF A BRIDE

To Thee, O God, I open my heart in prayer and thanksgiving. I rejoice in the love that has come to me to enrich my life. Thou hast blessed me with the devotion of a man who shall be my lifelong friend and companion. In all the vicissitudes of my life, I look to Thee for light and support, for help and guidance.

Be with me, O Father, as I strive to fulfil the manifold tasks of a true and devoted wife. May I learn to realize that more precious and enduring than grace and beauty are the tender words we speak and the kindly acts we do. Fill me with the spirit of the faithful daughters in Israel, who by their wisdom and virtue won the love, admiration and confidence of their husbands and children. Make me worthy of Thy blessings, and help me to build my home on the lasting foundations of love and truth and peace.

ON THE MARRIAGE OF A SON

"The mercy of the Lord is from everlasting
to everlasting; and His righteousness unto
children's children to such as keep His
covenant." *Psalm 103, 17, 18.*

O loving Father, Source of life, bounteous Giver
of blessing, what can I do to repay Thee for all
Thy bounties? I can only thank Thee for them and
for the happiness which fills my heart on the day
of the marriage of my beloved son. I recall Thy
constant goodness in the past years of his life from
the beginning to this day. How many were the
anxieties in the days which now have passed. Sickness and accidents, new and untried companions,
absence from home and the dangers of war have,
with Thy grace, all been surmounted. I thank
Thee with a parent's humble gratitude that Thou
hast protected and preserved him for himself and
for us and hast brought us in joy to this happy
day.

Now he stands at the threshold of a new life,
ready to establish his own home and to carry the
weight of adult duties. Be Thou with him, O God,
in all the years that lie ahead. Grant that the
ideals which now ennoble him remain with him
all his life. May his love for his dear bride never
fade but grow brighter through the years. May all
the tasks of life be shared by them together and

increase their sense of mutual loyalty and true comradeship.

May this union be blessed with children, a new generation which, with Thy grace, will grow in health and beauty of body and soul. May his new responsibilities bring him maturity so that self-reliant and strong he may become a useful and honored member of the community.

May all that we hoped to achieve in our own marriage be amply fulfilled in his. May his own hopes be blended with our prayers in the grand fulfillment of a noble home. AMEN.

ON THE MARRIAGE OF A DAUGHTER

"Blessed be thou of the Lord, my daughter."
Ruth 3, 10

To Thee, O Lord, I turn with prayers of thanksgiving for Thy manifold blessings in the years that have passed. All the tasks and the problems, the uncertainties and anxieties of many responsibilities are now richly rewarded by my joy in this happy day. She who was my infant baby, who grew to be my happy little girl and has matured into splendid young womanhood is about to be joined in marriage to the man of her choice. O accept the thankful thoughts of my heart that Thou hast granted me this blessed privilege to lead my daughter to the sheltering canopy of happy marriage.

With all my thanks to Thee, O God, come hopes and prayers for Thy renewed blessings. Be Thou with her in her new life which now begins. May the love which now beautifies her spirit never grow less. May this loving couple become truly comrades in life. May the family into which her husband was born become in understanding and love her own family, so that we and they be united into a larger company of friendship through the passing years.

Grant her unfailing health and increasing wisdom. May the children, which I pray you will grant her and her husband, bring them joy and pride. May she raise them with understanding and patient love. And grant, O God, that the home she will establish be one of the noble homes of Israel, illumined by the light of Thy presence and blessed with Thine unfailing love.   AMEN.

PRAYER IN BEHALF OF ONE IN CHILD-BIRTH

O Heavenly Father, Lord of all generations, Thou hast blest our life with comradeship and mutual love. I thank Thee for Thy manifold goodness in the past and pray for Thine aid in this time of waiting and anxiety.

O send Thy gracious help to my beloved one who now awaits the birth of our child. Grant her serenity of spirit that she may wait in confidence and calm. Bestow upon her strength of body and a heart unafraid. May the child be born to happy life and my dear wife be restored to perfect health. Bless us with the joys of worthy parenthood and with long life together in family love.   AMEN

PARENTAL PRAYER ON BIRTH OF A SON

O Lord, Source of all Life, we lift our hearts in thanks unto Thee for the life of the son whom Thou hast granted unto us and who has been entrusted by Thee to our care.

Bestow Thy blessing upon our little one. May he grow in strength of body, mind and spirit. May he develop in the love of Thee and of his fellowmen to the end that his life may glorify Thy name, be a blessing unto society, and a joy unto himself.

May the merits of the fathers and mothers in Israel rest upon him and guide him in paths pleasing in Thy sight.

Give unto us, O Father, the wisdom, courage, and faith that we as parents may perform our sacred duties in accordance with Thy will.   AMEN.

PARENTAL PRAYER ON BIRTH OF A DAUGHTER

Our Heavenly Father—Thou hast been exceedingly gracious unto us. From Thee unto us has come the life of our daughter. Our hearts are filled with gratitude. We would express our thanks not only with words but with our striving to do Thy will towards her whom Thou hast created in Thine image.

Be Thou her guide on life's path. Keep her life from all evil. Direct her spirit to the good, true and beautiful. May her life fulfill the ideal:

> "Grace is deceitful and beauty is vain, but a woman that feareth the Lord shall be praised."

Consecrate us, O God, to the responsibilities of parenthood and make us worthy of Thy love and mercy. AMEN.

CIRCUMCISION

Father:

In conformity with ancient and hallowed Jewish observance, I present my son for circumcision to bring him into the covenant of Abraham our father.

Praised be Thou, O Lord our God, Ruler of the world, who hast sanctified us with Thy commandments and enjoined upon us the rite of circumcision.

בָּרוּךְ אַתָּה יְהֹוָה אֱלֹהֵינוּ מֶלֶךְ הָעוֹלָם שֶׁהֶחֱיָנוּ וְקִיְּמָנוּ וְהִגִּיעָנוּ לַזְּמַן הַזֶּה:

Praised be Thou, O Lord our God, Ruler of the world, who hast granted us life, sustained us, and permitted us to witness this day in gladness and joy.

(Here the Circumcision is performed)

Father:

We praise Thee, O Lord, our God, in this hour in which a new born son has been brought into the covenant of Abraham. May this covenant be fulfilled in him by devotion to Thy law of truth and righteousness, by a marriage worthy of Thy blessing and by a life enriched with good deeds.

Be Thou, O God, with this child. Let him be known in Israel by the name _____.

Unto Thee, Heavenly Father, we lift our hearts in gratitude for Thy countless mercies. We thank Thee for this child who has entered into the covenant of Abraham. Send him Thy healing and bestow upon him Thy watchful care that he may grow to be a source of joy to his parents and to all his dear ones.

If Rabbi participates in the service, use the complete service in the Rabbi's Manual, pages 8–11.

PRAYER ON NAMING A CHILD

Praise and gratitude fill our hearts on this day
as we bring to Thee, Almighty God, the dear child
with which Thou hast blessed us. We dedicate it
to a life of usefulness, honor and piety. We bestow
upon it the name _____. May that name be
a token of every virtue. May Thy blessing attend
our dear child, to guard it against every evil, and
to keep it from every danger.

May it be worthy throughout life to be crowned
with Thy benediction: May God bless thee and
keep thee. May God let His countenance shine
upon thee, and be gracious unto thee. May God
lift up His countenance upon thee, and give thee
peace. AMEN.

יְבָרֶכְךָ יְיָ וְיִשְׁמְרֶךָ: יָאֵר יְיָ פָּנָיו
אֵלֶיךָ וִיחֻנֶּךָ: יִשָּׂא יְיָ פָּנָיו אֵלֶיךָ
וְיָשֵׂם לְךָ שָׁלוֹם:

ON ENTERING A CHILD IN RELIGIOUS SCHOOL

"These words which I command you this day
shall be upon thy heart . . . . and thou shalt
teach them diligently unto Thy children."
Deut. 6, 6–7

Eternal Father, Source of all knowledge, Guide
and Teacher of the generations of men: Thou
hast revealed Thyself unto Thy children in the
order and beauty of nature, in the promptings of
human conscience and in the loyal devotion of
sacred tradition. The knowledge of Thee is reborn
in the hearts and minds of all children. "Out of
the mouths of babes hast Thou established Thy
strength." Thou hast commanded us to foster this
natural knowledge of Thee, that it may grow
strong through knowledge, express itself in worship, and become ennobled through deeds of mercy
and justice to all Thy children.

As Hannah brought the child Samuel to learn
and serve in Thy house, as every older generation
brought its children to synagogue and school, as
my own beloved parents brought me into Thy
house that I may study Thy law, so do I now
bring my child to be enrolled among those who
seek to know Thy ways and to follow the path of
Thy commandments.

O God of Knowledge, grant, I pray Thee, that this child of mine grow in heart and mind. May the story of Thy guidance of the household of Israel, the discipline of the Law which they obeyed as Thy will, the mandate of righteousness which the prophets spoke in Thy name, all enter the life of my son (my daughter) that he (she) may be matured in knowledge and in the reverence of Thee. AMEN.

AT THE CONFIRMATION OF A CHILD

"And all thy children shall be taught
of the Lord."   *Isaiah 54, 13.*

Eternal Father, our lives are in Thy hand and
our souls are in Thy keeping. Humbly do I thank
Thee this day that Thou hast given health and
growth to my beloved son (daughter). Thou hast
shielded him (her) during infancy; in the growing
years Thou hast strengthened him (her) and hast
brought him (her) in health to the threshold of
adult life. Now he (she) stands at Thy sacred altar
to be confirmed in the faith of Israel and I voice my
gratitude in the ancient words:—

"Praised be Thou, O Lord our God, King of
the Universe, that Thou hast kept us alive
and sustained us to this great day."

O Lord, hearken to the voice of my heart as I
pray for this child of mine. Grant that this day's
service be as a crowning glory to all his (her) years
of religious instruction. May it engrave on the
tablets of his (her) heart the wondrous story of Thy
guidance of Israel who in a world of idol-worship
and ignorance came to the knowledge of Thee and
Thy truth. May the exalted teachings of Thy
prophets move him (her) to deeds of justice and of
loving kindness to all. May the recollection of this

day inspire him (her) to seek Thy presence in the worship of Thee in the congregation of Thy faithful children.

O Lord, as Thou dost bless him (her), guide Thou my life also, that I may be a worthy parent to a noble child. Awaken in me the strength to do Thy will in all my dealings with my fellowman. May the anxieties and distractions of daily living never estrange me from Thee, O Father. May our home be consecrated to Thee, and for the years which Thou will grant us together, may my child and I seek Thee in worship side by side. This day strengthen us. Give us this day Thy blessing. AMEN.

Prayers for Night and Morning
for
Adults and Children

A.   NIGHT PRAYER FOR CHILDREN

I thank Thee, O God, for the blessings of this day. Thou art my Shepherd; I shall not want. Thou dost neither sleep nor slumber. I fear no evil, for Thou art with me; in peace, I lay me down to sleep. Bless my home, and all who are dear to me.

שְׁמַע יִשְׂרָאֵל יְהֹוָה אֱלֹהֵינוּ יְהֹוָה אֶחָד:

Hear, O Israel, the Lord our God, the Lord is One.

בָּרוּךְ שֵׁם כְּבוֹד מַלְכוּתוֹ לְעוֹלָם וָעֶד:

Blessed be His name, whose glorious kingdom is forever and ever.

בְּיָדוֹ אַפְקִיד רוּחִי. בְּעֵת אִישַׁן וְאָעִירָה:
לִישׁוּעָתְךָ קִוִּיתִי יְיָ:

I am in Thy care, O God, when I sleep and when I wake. In Thy help I trust, O Lord. AMEN.

B.   *Or the following:*

Now the hours of day are over
I thank Thee, Lord, for all Thy good,
For father's care and gentle mother
Who guard and give me daily food.

Thy quiet stars keep watch above me,
I lay me down to slumber deep.
Guard Thou, O God, all those who love me,
Wake me again from restful sleep.

Sh'ma Yis-ro-el A-do-noy Elo-he-nu, A-do-noy
E-chod.

Hear, O Israel, the Lord our God, the Lord is One.
AMEN.

C. *Or the following:*

For the day and my play,
I thank Thee, O God, in every way,
Through the night and my rest,
Thy love keep me and bless.

Sh'ma Yis-ro-el, A-do-noy Elo-he-nu, A-do-noy
E-chod.

Hear, O Israel, the Lord our God, the Lord is One.

Bless my dear ＿＿＿＿＿＿ and all Thy children.
AMEN.

MORNING PRAYER FOR ADULTS

Almighty God, I thank Thee that Thou hast permitted me to wake to the light of a new day.

(I thank Thee, O God:

For the Sabbath with its message of rest to strengthen faith in Thee.

For the New Year and Atonement Days, which teach me of Thy great mercy.

For the Festivals, which remind me of Thy kindness to our forefathers.)

Thy goodness, which is without end, has given me the quiet of refreshing sleep, and has quickened me with the energy of new life.

Withdraw not Thy hand from me; let Thy love be near me. Let all my thoughts, words and deeds be acceptable in Thy sight. Grant that this day, which I receive as a gift from Thee, may not be spent in vain. Strengthen my soul, that I may be of service to my fellow-men.

Let me walk before Thee in humility. Aid me to overcome temptation. May my heart be filled with reverence and love for Thee. May I trust steadfastly in the wisdom and goodness of Thine all-ruling will.

שְׁמַע יִשְׂרָאֵל יְהֹוָה אֱלֹהֵינוּ יְהֹוָה אֶחָד:

Hear, O Israel, the Lord our God, the Lord is One.

בָּרוּךְ שֵׁם כְּבוֹד מַלְכוּתוֹ לְעוֹלָם וָעֶד:

Blessed be His name, whose glorious kingdom is forever and ever.

וְאָהַבְתָּ אֵת יְהֹוָה אֱלֹהֶיךָ בְּכָל־לְבָבְךָ וּבְכָל־
נַפְשְׁךָ וּבְכָל־מְאֹדֶךָ:

Thou shalt love the Lord, thy God, with all thy heart, with all thy soul, and with all thy might.

B.   Give me the strength to meet each day
With quiet will.
Give me the faith to know Thou art
My Shepherd still.
Give me the light to find my way
When shadows fall.
Be Thou my steady, guiding star,
Father of all!

שְׁמַע יִשְׂרָאֵל יְהֹוָה אֱלֹהֵינוּ יְהֹוָה אֶחָד:

Hear, O Israel, the Lord our God, the Lord is One.

C.   Creator of the Universe, the heavens declare Thy glory and the firmament showeth Thy handi-work. We see Thy love in the light of the rising sun which dispels evening's darkness, and brings warmth and radiance into the lives of all Thy children. Make us to understand that even so does faith dispel the clouds of despair, and Thy benign love penetrate the shades of sorrow. Lift our eyes to behold the wonders of Thy creation, that every day we sing a new song of gladness for this wondrous world over which Thou hast given man domination. AMEN.

D. Bless the Lord, O my soul, and all that is within me, bless His holy Name. I thank Thee, Lord, that Thou hast renewed my breath within me this morning, and that my being is awake to the wonders of Thy creation. The heavens declare Thy glory and the firmanent showeth Thy handiwork. Help me, O Lord, to make my fellowmen sing Thy praises through this day, by being a friend to them, as Thou art my Friend. Let me walk by their side, and enable me to dispel their fears and to relieve their anxieties. May I show them the brightness of goodness, the wonder of love and the power of righteousness; for these gifts come from Thy hands— and I would use them for Thy glory. AMEN.

שְׁמַע יִשְׂרָאֵל יְהֹוָה אֱלֹהֵינוּ יְהֹוָה אֶחָד׃

Hear, O Israel, the Lord our God, the Lord is One.

NIGHT PRAYER FOR ADULTS

A

O God, as this day closes, humbly I thank Thee for all that it has brought me; for its joys and also for its trials; for earnest efforts, sweet affection and uplifting hopes.

Grant that my deeds may show that I am worthy of Thy favor. Strengthen me, O God, that I may love Thee with all my heart, with all my soul and with all my might. Pardon, O Father, my shortcomings. Help me to forgive all who may have wronged me; and grant me strength to seek pardon of all whom I may have offended.

O God, Thou who dost neither sleep nor slumber, spread over me the shelter of Thy peace; guard my home and all dear to me. Yea, may Thy blessing of peace rest upon all Thy children.

שְׁמַע יִשְׂרָאֵל יְהֹוָה אֱלֹהֵינוּ יְהֹוָה אֶחָד׃

Hear, O Israel, the Lord our God, the Lord is One.

בָּרוּךְ שֵׁם כְּבוֹד מַלְכוּתוֹ לְעוֹלָם וָעֶד׃

Blessed be His name, whose glorious kingdom is forever and ever.

בְּיָדוֹ אַפְקִיד רוּחִי. בְּעֵת אִישַׁן וְאָעִירָה:
וְעִם רוּחִי גְּוִיָּתִי. יְיָ לִי וְלֹא אִירָא:

I am in Thy care, O God, when I sleep and
when I wake.

My body and my soul are Thine. Thou art with
me, I will not fear.

B

When in sleep I close my eyes,
To Thee, O God, my prayers arise.
Help me to sleep throughout the night
And strengthened feel at morning light.

MORNING PRAYER FOR CHILDREN

Blessed art Thou, O Lord our God, Father of
all, for letting me wake to this new day. O God,
be with me always, that I may be loving to my
parents and dear ones. Help me to be kind to all.
May I willingly obey those who teach me. Lead
me in Thy paths of truth. Help me to be faithful
to all my duties.

שְׁמַע יִשְׂרָאֵל יְהֹוָה אֱלֹהֵינוּ יְהֹוָה אֶחָד:

Hear, O Israel, the Lord our God, the Lord is
One.

בָּרוּךְ שֵׁם כְּבוֹד מַלְכוּתוֹ לְעוֹלָם וָעֶד:

Blessed be His name, whose glorious kingdom is forever and ever.

וְאָהַבְתָּ אֵת יְהֹוָה אֱלֹהֶיךָ בְּכָל־לְבָבְךָ וּבְכָל־
נַפְשְׁךָ וּבְכָל־מְאֹדֶךָ:

Thou shalt love the Lord, thy God, with all thy heart, with all thy soul, and with all thy might.

Prayers in Time of Sickness and Death

PRAYER IN TIME OF TROUBLE

All-wise ruler of the destinies of man, out of the depths of my sorrow I cry unto Thee. Thou hast laid upon me a heavy burden and tried me with sorrow. Days of anguish and nights of weeping hast Thou meted out to me. Humbly I bow beneath Thy decree and try to accept Thy will. For what am I, but dust and ashes, that I should murmur against the wisdom of Thy ways? I feel that Thy decrees, though hard to bear, are meant for good and not for evil.

In the gloom around me, I look to Thee for light. Let me not seek in vain for Thy sustaining arm. Let me not rebel at Thy chastening, O Lord. Redeem me from faults and grant me strength to do Thy will with a perfect heart.   AMEN.

PRAYERS IN SICKNESS

Prayer Said by the Sick During Illness

O God, I am sorely stricken; but in my pain let me not forget Thee. Thou art long-suffering and patient; and in Thy great mercy Thou wilt forgive the murmuring lips and the weary soul. Give me understanding to know that this bitter trial has come upon me for my welfare, that I may not despise Thy chastening.

In all humility I lay bare my soul before Thee and ask Thy pardon for my shortcomings. A broken and contrite heart Thou wilt not despise.

May it be Thy will to aid those who would bring me to a speedy recovery. I thank Thee for all the dear ones whose sympathy and care have eased my suffering. Mayest Thou answer the prayers of our hearts. Heal me, that I may again praise Thy name in the congregation of Israel.

Psalm xx

The Lord answer Thee in the day of trouble;
The name of the God of Jacob set thee up on high;
Send forth thy help from the sanctuary,
And support thee out of Zion;
Grant thee according to thine own heart, and
    fulfil all thy counsel.

Now know I that the Lord saveth His anointed;
He will answer him from His holy heaven,
With the mighty acts of His saving right hand.
Some trust in chariots, and some in horses;
But we will make mention of the name of the Lord
    our God
Save, Lord;
Let the King answer us in the day that we call.

PSALM LVI

In God do I trust, I will not be afraid;
What can man do unto me?
I will render thank-offerings unto Thee.
For Thou hast delivered my soul from death
Thou hast delivered my feet from stumbling.

O rejoice the soul of Thy servant, for unto Thee,
O Lord, do I lift up mine eyes. Heal me, O Lord,
and I shall be healed; save me and I shall be saved,
for Thou art my praise. AMEN.

PSALM CIII

Bless the Lord, O my soul, and all that is within
    me, bless His holy name.
Bless the Lord, O my soul, and forget not all His
    benefits:

He forgiveth all thine iniquities; He healeth all thy diseases;

He redeemeth thy life from destruction; He crowneth thee with kindness and mercies;

He satisfieth with good thine old age so that thy youth is renewed like the eagle.

The Lord executeth righteousness and justice for all that are oppressed.

Merciful and gracious is the Lord, long-suffering, and abundant in kindness.

As for man, his days are as grass: as the flower of the field so he flourisheth.

When a wind but passeth over it, it is gone, and its place shall know it no more.

But the kindness of the Lord is from everlasting to everlasting over those that fear Him, and His righteousness unto children's children,

To such as keep His covenant, and those who remember His precepts, to obey them.

Bless ye the Lord, all His works, in all places of His dominion: bless the Lord, O my soul.

PRAYER SAID BY THE SICK ON RECOVERY

O my God, Father of Mercy, I thank Thee for the healing which Thy lovingkindness has wrought for me. Thou hast raised me from a bed of sickness. When I was racked with pain, when my strength was spent and my very soul within me trembled, Thou didst not forsake me. Thou hast saved me, keeping me in the land of the living, restoring me to health and the sweet companionship of my beloved ones.

With great rejoicing therefore, and with all my soul, I bring to Thee the offering of my thanksgiving. Help me so to use my renewed strength that I may be of service to Thee by being a blessing to my fellow men. AMEN.

PSALM XXX

I will extol Thee, O Lord, for Thou hast lifted me up, and hast not made my foes to rejoice over me.

O Lord, my God, I cried unto Thee, and Thou hast healed me.

I had said in my prosperity, I shall never be moved.
    O Lord, in Thy favor, Thou hadst set up for me a mountain of strength; then Thou didst hide Thy face, and lo, I was stricken with terror.

Unto Thee, O Lord, did I cry, and unto my Lord
I made supplication.

And so Thou didst turn my mourning into dancing.
Thou hast loosed my sackcloth, and girded me
with gladness.

That my glory may sing praise unto Thee, and
not be silent. O Lord, my God, I will give
thanks unto Thee forevermore.

PRAYER SAID FOR THE SICK

O God, Healer of the sick, unto Thee I humbly direct my petition. Not because of righteousness or merit in myself, but because of Thine abundant mercy, I offer unto Thee my supplications.

My soul is in anguish because of the illness of my dear _____ ; and in this hour of fear and anxiety my heart turns to Thee.

May it be Thy will to grant a speedy recovery. O Father of life, I pray Thee, grant renewed strength and length of days.

Bless the endeavors of all who bring help unto the sick. Strengthen me that I may bring cheer and comfort unto the suffering one.

Do Thou, O gracious God, enable me to bear patiently the decrees of Thy Providence. Arouse me from despondency. Help me to know that Thy thoughts are not our thoughts and Thy ways are not our ways.   AMEN.

PSALM CIII

Bless the Lord, O my soul, and all that is within me, bless His Holy name.

Bless the Lord, O my soul, and forget not all His benefits.

Psalm cxvi

I love that the Lord should hear
My voice and my supplications.
Because He hath inclined His ear unto me,
Therefore will I call upon Him all my days.

I found trouble and sorrow.
But I called upon the name of the Lord:
'I beseech Thee, O Lord, deliver my soul'.
Gracious is the Lord, and righteous,
Yea, our God is compassionate.
The Lord preserveth the simple;
I was brought low, and He saved me.

Return, O my soul, unto thy rest;
For the Lord hath dealt bountifully with thee
For Thou hast delivered my soul from death,
Mine eyes from tears,
And my feet from stumbling.
I shall walk before the Lord
In the lands of the living.
I trusted even when I spoke:
'I am greatly afflicted'.

ON VISITING A CEMETERY

The Lord is nigh unto the broken in heart. He saveth them that are of contrite spirit. Many are the afflictions of the righteous, yet the Lord delivereth him out of them all.

The Lord redeemeth the soul of His servants, none shall be condemned that trust in Him.

O Eternal Father, Thou keepest faith with Thy children in death as in life. Thou dost grant us the privilege of living in the service of Thee and dost bestow upon us eternal peace when our toils on earth are ended. I thank Thee for the blessed life of my loved one who has here been laid to rest. For the joy of companionship, for the sharing of happiness and sorrow, for the plans and achievements and even the shared disappointments, for all of them, I humbly praise Thy name.

I come now to pay homage to this beloved memory. Grant to my dear one eternal peace and may he (she) be a light unto my path and a blessing day by day. AMEN.

AT THE GRAVE OF A FATHER

Here, in the rest and peace of this hallowed spot, I wait patiently for Thy help, O God, for I seek Thee with my whole heart.

Thou, O God, didst give unto me many blessings in the life of my dear father. His strong love for home and dear ones; his faithful, untiring efforts to make comfort, happiness and peace dwell under our roof; his constant solicitude for the health of my body and the growth of my soul; yea, all these memories flood my mind and overflow often into tears of heavy sorrow.

Yet, Thou, O Eternal Father of all creation, knowest that my grief is not of rebellion against Thy mysterious decrees. For the sigh that leaves my lips when I think of my great loss also breathes the thankfulness of my heart for the blessing my father's life was to me.

O God, in whose keeping, in death as in life, are the souls of all, I thank Thee for the many noble impulses that come to me here from the memories of my dear father's life. As he gave unto me the crown of a good name, may I, in leaving this hallowed spot, resolve to keep pure that good name and cherish it more than the most precious of earthly treasures.   AMEN.

KADDISH (Page 91)

AT THE GRAVE OF A MOTHER

With the spirit of trustfulness in my heart, I approach Thee, O God, at the grave of my dearly beloved mother.

Days, months and many years pass away. Innumerable are the blessings which Thy mercies provide. O may these sustain me amid all the changes of time, in the hours of sadness and loneliness.

Drawn by the tender memories of a mother's love, and the deathless ties of filial affection, I come to this consecrated spot to pour out my heart in prayer. As I recall my mother's patient love and her prayers for my welfare, my heart is heavy and my voice is silenced with grief. O God, help me to consecrate my sorrow to Thee.

May the memory of my mother inspire me with deeper love for life; and the faith that she is in Thine eternal keeping, strengthen my soul. I return to my home and to the living, resolved to fulfil every duty to myself and to my fellow men, nobly and well. I will be faithful to Thee, O God; I will befriend the motherless, the orphan, the widow, the poor and the stranger.

May the words of my mouth and the meditations of my heart be acceptable in Thy sight, O God, my strength and my redeemer. AMEN.

KADDISH (page 91)

AT THE GRAVE OF A HUSBAND

O Loving God, behold the sorrow of my heart. Widowed and bereft I mourn the loss of the dear companion of my life.

Help me, O God, to bear this burden bravely. Teach me to bend my will to Thy supreme will that doeth all things for the best; for all Thy ways are right and all Thy judgments just. Thou didst send me untold blessings through the gift of his loving care. For these my heart overflows with thankfulness. May I not mar the gratitude I here offer by murmurs and complaints.

Grant that I may live true to the hopes and prayers which bound our hearts together. Fill me with zeal to carry out every noble thought he cherished, and to fulfil every duty to my home and my dear ones which he bequeathed to me. May the memory of his love and faithfulness ever aid and inspire me.

I cast my burden upon Thee, O Lord. Uphold me in the hours of my weakness, for Thou art near to the broken and contrite heart. May my life prove that love is as strong as death. Grant more and more of the comforting faith in life immortal. May Thy blessing of peace attend me throughout all my days.   AMEN.

KADDISH (page 91)

AT THE GRAVE OF A WIFE

My heart cries unto Thee, Almighty God, out of the depths of my distress. Thou alone knowest the loneliness of my days, bereft of her whom Thou gavest me as my companion and helpmate. Here in this narrow home I have placed to rest with her much of my own life, and naught remains to me but the precious memory of her tenderness and her devotion. Let me not yield to despair. Help me to be loyal to every trust she reposed in me, and steadfast to every duty her passing away has left to me. Fill me with manly courage to live true to the ideals of purity and nobility with which she inspired me.

Grant unto me strength, and unto our dear ones the steadfast resolve to cherish faithfully the spirit of love with which she filled our home. May the example of her goodness live on as an impulse to every good endeavor. May the bonds of our common sorrow unite more firmly the ties of our family affections. Teach me, O God, the lesson of resignation. Fill me with the firm trust that death does not end all; but that in death, as in life, all are in Thy keeping. May I say with sincere humility: "Thy thoughts are not our thoughts; nor are Thy ways our ways. For high as are the heavens above the earth, so high are Thy ways above our ways, and Thy thoughts above our thoughts." AMEN.

KADDISH (Page 91)

AT THE GRAVE OF A BROTHER

Tender memories fill my thoughts as I stand here by the grave of my brother. Precious was the blessing that God gave me in his life. A brother, indeed, was he at all times, kind and considerate in his words, thoughtful and generous in his deeds.

O God, in Thine infinite wisdom and justice Thou hast taken him from me. I sorely miss him. But the influence of his character is and ever shall be upon me. I pray Thee, O God, to strengthen my soul with an abiding faith in life hereafter; and give me courage to bear whatever Thy Providence sends unto me. According to my power, may I never fail to aid others who are in need of sympathy and help. AMEN.

KADDISH (Page 91)

AT THE GRAVE OF A SISTER

How precious to me was the deep love of my sister! And now, O God, that Thou hast taken her from me there is a void which I often feel can never be filled.

Her kindness, her patience, her comforting words softened the trials of many a day. As I think of all this, how heavily is my heart bowed down by the sorrow of her taking away.

As I stand in the peaceful quiet of this spot, divine hope whispers in my soul that she is at rest in Thy keeping. May this thought sustain me. May I be thankful unto Thee, O God, for the life of my dear sister; and may every thought of her incline my soul to deeds of kindness, mercy, and righteousness. AMEN.

KADDISH (Page 91)

AT THE GRAVE OF A CHILD

O God, from the depths I cry unto Thee. Thou hast taken away from me my dear child. O help me to feel that the ways of Thy Providence are wise and good, though we understand them not.

Thou, O God, knowest that my soul would not question Thy justice; I would not rebel against Thy decree. It is the tender and deep love which my dear child brought into my heart that draws me hither. And so, O merciful Father, have mercy upon me, and send the healing balm of Thy consolation to my grieving spirit.

In this moment my spirit has but little strength to praise. Yet if Thou didst take away this life, Thou also didst give it. O may the light of love which my child kindled within my heart, continue to burn brightly, so that, as I regain strength of soul, I may bring cheer unto all my dear ones. Blessed be Thou, O God, who comfortest the mourner with hope in life eternal. AMEN.

KADDISH (Page 91)

AT THE GRAVE OF A RELATIVE

I stand by the grave of my dear ———— feeling the burden of the last parting on earth; and I would lift up my heart in prayer unto Thee, O God, who givest life and takest it away.

I thank Thee, O God, for the ties that united my ———— and me in life; for the watchful interest in my welfare, the ready sympathy, and the many deeds of lovingkindness which bound our souls with the lasting cords of family love.

Now, O God, that Thou, in Thine infinite justice and wisdom hast called my dear _____ hence, I cherish these memories; and I think of the departed soul as in Thy keeping among the righteous.

Though the bonds of affection are severed, yet strong as death is the devotion of my heart. And in this hour, at this grave, I would renew the sweet sentiments that bound us in life, and dedicate them unto the service of my fellow men. May Thy peace, O God, abide with us in life and in death. AMEN.

KADDISH (Page 91)

AT THE GRAVE OF A FRIEND

I have come to this sacred spot drawn by the eternal ties that bound fast the soul of my dear friend unto mine. Death, alas, has separated us. Days and years come and go, and this deep sorrow Thou alone, O God, in Thy mercy canst heal in the passing of time.

Life, with its continuous round of duties, its trying moments, its joys and sorrows, does not find my friend near me as of yore to share my confidence, to encourage my hopes, to enter into my disappointments and to partake of my joys. My soul grieves sorely for this loss.

Mysterious as is Thy final decree, O God, yet I will not be unmindful of Thy gracious gift of our friendship. May its divine blessing abide with me so that my life may reveal the lovingkindness which Thou, O our Heavenly Father, dost show unto all Thy creatures. Blessed be Thou, O God, for the immortal soul within us.   AMEN.

KADDISH (Page 91)

AT THE GRAVE OF A TEACHER

I have come to this, the last resting-place on earth of my dear teacher, to recall before Thee, O God, the blessings with which he enriched my life.

The strength of his gentle character, the example of his reverence, of his love for wisdom and truth, and all the grateful memories of his life, bring me hither to pay this simple tribute of love. His labors, that brought the knowledge of God's law unto so many souls, shall ever help me to make my life acceptable in Thy sight, O God. May I be true to his teachings by pointing unto others through word and deed the path of eternal life he showed unto me.   AMEN.

KADDISH (Page 91)

AT THE GRAVE OF A GREAT PERSON

"The Lord is near to all who call upon Him; who call upon Him in truth." This thought of the Psalmist fills me as I stand by this memorial of greatness. In all ages, Thou, O God, hast inspired men and women in all places of this earth to endure and struggle, to the end that life may be enriched with art and knowledge; that the soul may be exalted through ideals of charity, of hope and of faith.

May the devotion of such great souls to Thy work, O God, inspire me to a life of more and more usefulness in Thy sight; and may my soul ever be open to all truth.

May these words of prayer be acceptable unto Thee, O God, in whose keeping are the righteous of all peoples forever and ever. AMEN.

KADDISH (Page 91)

MOURNER'S PRAYER

Extolled and hallowed be the name of God throughout the world which He has created, and which He governs according to His righteous will. Just is He in all His ways, and wise are all His decrees. May His kingdom come, and His will be done in all the earth.

Blessed be the Lord of life, the righteous Judge for evermore.

To the departed whom we now remember, may peace and bliss be granted in the world of eternal life. There may they find grace and mercy before the Lord of heaven and earth. May their souls rejoice in that ineffable good which God has laid up for those that fear Him, and may their memory be a blessing unto those that cherish it.

May the Father of peace send peace to all troubled souls, and comfort all the bereaved among us.   AMEN.

KADDISH

יִתְגַּדַּל וְיִתְקַדַּשׁ שְׁמֵהּ רַבָּא. בְּעָלְמָא דִי־בְרָא
כִרְעוּתֵהּ. וְיַמְלִיךְ מַלְכוּתֵהּ. בְּחַיֵּיכוֹן וּבְיוֹמֵיכוֹן
וּבְחַיֵּי דְכָל בֵּית יִשְׂרָאֵל. בַּעֲגָלָא וּבִזְמַן קָרִיב.
וְאִמְרוּ אָמֵן:

יְהֵא שְׁמֵהּ רַבָּא מְבָרַךְ. לְעָלַם וּלְעָלְמֵי עָלְמַיָּא:

יִתְבָּרַךְ וְיִשְׁתַּבַּח וְיִתְפָּאַר וְיִתְרוֹמַם וְיִתְנַשֵּׂא
וְיִתְהַדָּר וְיִתְעַלֶּה וְיִתְהַלָּל שְׁמֵהּ דְּקוּדְשָׁא. בְּרִיךְ
הוּא. לְעֵלָּא מִן כָּל בִּרְכָתָא וְשִׁירָתָא. תֻּשְׁבְּחָתָא
וְנֶחֱמָתָא. דַּאֲמִירָן בְּעָלְמָא. וְאִמְרוּ אָמֵן:

עַל יִשְׂרָאֵל וְעַל צַדִּיקַיָּא. וְעַל־כָּל־מַן
דְּאִתְפְּטַר מִן עָלְמָא הָדֵין כִּרְעוּתֵהּ דֶאֱלָהָא. יְהֵא
לְהוֹן שְׁלָמָא רַבָּא וְחוּלָקָא טָבָא לְחַיֵּי עָלְמָא דְּאָתֵי.
וְחִסְדָּא וְרַחֲמֵי מִן־קֳדָם מָרֵא שְׁמַיָּא וְאַרְעָא.
וְאִמְרוּ אָמֵן:

יְהֵא שְׁלָמָא רַבָּא מִן־שְׁמַיָּא וְחַיִּים. עָלֵינוּ וְעַל־
כָּל־יִשְׂרָאֵל. וְאִמְרוּ אָמֵן:

עֹשֶׂה שָׁלוֹם בִּמְרוֹמָיו. הוּא יַעֲשֶׂה שָׁלוֹם עָלֵינוּ
וְעַל כָּל יִשְׂרָאֵל. וְאִמְרוּ אָמֵן:

THE MOURNER'S KADDISH

Mourner

Yis-gad-dal v'yis-kad-dash sh'meh rab-bo, b'ol-mo di-'vro kir'-u-seh v'yam-lich mal-chu-seh, b'cha-ye-chon u-v'yo-me-chon u-v'cha-yeh d'chol bes yis-ro-el, ba-a-go-lo u-viz-man ko-riv, v'im-ru: O-men.

Y'heh sh'meh rab-bo m'vo-rach, l'o-lam ul'-ol-meh ol-ma-yo.

Yis-bo-rach, v'yish-tab-bach, v'yis-po-ar, v'yis-ro-mam, v'yis-nas-seh, v'yis-had-dor, v'yis-al-leh, v'yis-hal-lol, sh'meh d'kud'-sho, b'rich hu. L'e-lo min kol bir-cho-so, v'shi-ro-so, tush-b'cho-so, v'ne-ch'-mo-so, da-a-mi-ron b'ol-mo, v'im-ru: O-men.

Al yis-ro-el v'al tsa-de-ka-yo, v'al kol man d'isp'tar min ol-mo ho-dain kir-ooseh de-e-lo-ho, y'hai l'hon shlo-mo rab-bo v'chino v'chis-do min ko-dom mo-rai sh'ma-yo v'ar-o, v'im-ru: O-men.

Y'heh sh'lo-mo rab-bo min sh'ma-yo v'cha-yim, o-le-nu v'al kol yis-ro-el, v'im-ru: O-men.

O-seh sho-lom bim'-ro-mov, hu ya-a-seh, sho-lom, o-le-nu v'al kol yis-ro-el, v'im-ru: O-men.

Meditations

INDEX TO MEDITATIONS

Morning Prayer

I lay me down and I sleep, I awake for the Lord sustaineth me. Give ear to my words, O Lord, consider my meditation. O Lord in the morning will I order my prayer unto Thee, and will look forward.

Psalms 3, 6; 5, 2, 4.

At the dawn I seek Thee, Refuge, Rock sublime,
Set my prayers before Thee in the morning
And my prayer at eventime.
I, before Thy greatness, stand and am afraid.
All my secret thoughts Thine eye beholdeth,
Deep within my bosom laid.

Solomon ibn Gabirol, 12th Century (Translated by Nina Salaman).

The simple tasks of every day require energy and faith. Daily duty with its inevitable repetition becomes irksome, and joyous tasks gradually turn into halfhearted toil. Time dampens our enthusiasm and in our weariness we begin to doubt the value of our labors. The routine of life saps the energies, dulls the courage and weakens faith.

In order that man continue his work in patience and in strength, he must try to infuse the spirit of creative joy into the routine of his common tasks. Our fathers understood this necessity for daily inspiration, and therefore they conceived of themselves as laboring in a great cause. God, they said, was their Employer and they labored in His workshop fulfilling His mighty plans. They strengthened themselves with the assurance that any man, if he be patient, true and brave, may become the co-worker of God Himself in the creation and the maintenance of the world.

The unfailing strength of such an ideal is waiting for every man who seeks it. When man emerges every morning from the mystery of sleep into the bright daylight of waking life, let him begin the day with thanks to the God of all men, for life restored and strength renewed. Before he begins his daily tasks let him spend a moment in contemplation of the work of the divine Artisan who renews daily the wonders of His creation. Let him pray humbly for a share of the infinite creative power.

If man will begin his task with the reverent consciousness of God's presence, then even his humblest achievement will be holy unto the Lord. If man will strive with the beginning of each day to make the day's work acceptable to God, then even if he fall short of full achievement, and even if his fellowmen deem his work to have failed, he will have succeeded in the sight of God, who sees the hearts of men.

Master of the world, mighty Creator, how manifold are Thy works. In wisdom hast Thou created them, and in lovingkindness dost Thou constantly maintain them. Into our frail hearts hast Thou breathed Thy spirit, inspiring us to toil, and teaching us to worship Thee by the work of our hands. We thank Thee, O Father, for the impulse to labor; for the tasks which call upon our powers, for the countless opportunities to continue Thy creative work. We thank Thee for those moments of joy when we can look upon the work of our hands and truly say: Behold it is good.

Heavenly Master, at the dawn of a new day, hear my voice. Thou art the source of my strength. Unless Thou build the house, in vain do I toil. Without Thy presence I lose faith in my strength, my courage ebbs and difficulties defeat me. Before the toil of the day begins, I lay before Thee the meditations of my heart. May they be acceptable in Thy sight. I commend the results of my labor into Thy hands; may they be deemed worthy of Thine approval. Grant me, O divine Source of strength, the power to toil patiently and to hope for Thy blessing. May this day bring me nearer to Thee. AMEN.

The Changing World

Blessed be the Lord, day by day He beareth our burden, even the God who is our salvation.

Surely the Lord's mercies are not consumed. Surely, His compassions fail not. They are new every morning.

Turn us unto Thee, O Lord,—renew our days as of old.

Psalm 68, 20; Lamentations 3, 22–24; 5, 21.

Praised be Thou who in Thy goodness renewest each day the wonders of creation.

The Prayerbook.

Toil would be purposeless if the world were unchangeable. If there is nothing new under the sun, then what profit lies in all our work? If there is nothing that we can change, what can we hope to accomplish? In reality no two things are exactly alike. No two days, no two hours, no two minutes are exactly alike. With every passing moment, the entire world changes. God constantly creates a new heaven and a new earth. The world is incessantly different from what it has been. The world is always new.

When once we perceive the vision of the changing world, our spiritual mood is transformed. We are chastened and also strengthened for there is both a solemn and a cheering implication in this thought.

Its solemn implication is that we may never rest from labor. We must ever be up and doing, for no achievement is final. Yesterday's attainments may have been suited to yesterday's world, but today the world is re-made and different. Since it is a new world, behold there is a new work to do, new temptations to resist, new problems to solve! There can be no resting on our laurels, no folding of our hands, no luxuriating in the thought of the victory won.

The living variation of days and years, the endless changing of the world, has also a cheering implication. It proclaims that a new world is a world of fresh beginning and new opportunities. The world of yesterday's discouragements is no longer the world that we are living in today. Yesterday we may have lost the battle but today we fight anew—perhaps to win. We blundered yesterday. But the blunder may be remedied; because yesterday's world with its errors and missteps has passed. Today's page is sufficiently clean, ready to receive the writing of a new endeavor.

Heavenly Father, Everpresent Power, whose creative work is endless, the ancient days of creation were but the beginning of Thy work. When Thou openest mine eyes to Thy power, I behold Thee maintaining the world, dwelling within it and renewing it daily with Thy love.

Thy constant presence, O Lord, is my strength. Since Thou art near, I call upon Thee, and pray that Thou renew my failing heart as Thou renewest daily Thy wondrous works. Grant me new courage with the new day.

O assure me that yesterday's reverses have not broken me, that they have only given me added knowledge wherewith to grasp my problems more firmly; and that during the pause of the night, Thou hast granted me wisdom and strength. May Thy presence in my heart be my shield and buckler as I start the battle afresh. This day, be it of defeat or of victory—may it be Thy day, O Lord. Create in me a stronger yearning for Thy presence so that, chance what will, I shall draw closer unto Thee, learning to know Thee with a fuller knowledge and to love Thee with a deeper and deeper love. AMEN.

The Soul of the World

The heavens declare the glory of God, and the firmament showeth His handiwork. Day unto day uttereth speech, and night unto night revealeth knowledge. There is no speech, there are no words, neither is their voice heard. Their line is gone out through all the earth, and their words to the end of the world.

Bless the Lord, O my soul. O Lord my God, Thou art very great; Thou art clothed with glory and majesty. Who coverest Thyself with light as with a garment, who stretchest out the heavens like a curtain; who layest the beams of Thine upper chambers in the waters, who makest the clouds Thy chariot, who walkest upon the wings of the wind; who makest winds Thy messengers, the flaming fire Thy ministers.

Psalms 19, 2–5; 104, 1–4.

There are men who boast of their deeds, doing little and saying much. There are men who, when they work, sound loud bells so that the report of their goodness be heard afar. To such, the heavens have no voice.

Isaac Arama, 15th Century (Adapted from Akeda I, 13b).

When the soul meditates upon the greatness of His might and His transcendant power, it bows before Him in awe and trembling. Then fear gives way to trust in Him, until the soul finds rest from

all its terrors, and longs for the cup of God's love
seeking to unite with Him in faith and yearning.
Bachya, "Duties of the Heart", 11th Century
(Gate of Love, I).

We frequently realize that it is only the surface
of life that we see. We are vaguely aware of the
spiritual laws imbedded in the plan of life, but we
do not easily perceive them. For while obvious
facts sound loudly in our ears, the soul of the world
rests in silence. It does not clamor for our attention;
there is no sound of it; its voice is not easily heard.
The material facts of the world obtrude themselves upon us, but in order to find the spirit of the
universe, we must earnestly seek. We must not
expect sudden revelations. Indeed great truths
frequently come in a flash of light, but only to those
who have been bravely groping in the darkness.

God is within and all about us, yet we plod on
in the daily round of life unaware of ever-present
divinity. But if we summon our power to search
for Him in our own experiences, in the souls of
men, in the mysteries of nature, He will graciously
cause the light of His countenance to shine upon us,
and we will perceive at last, if only faintly, all of
nature revealing His glory, the heavens to the earth,
the east unto the west, and day unto day.

Lord of all worlds, the heaven is Thy throne;
Thou inhabitest eternity. Far beyond my feeble

sight, Thou dwellest in majesty. O God of Knowledge, Thou hast implanted within me a sense of
Thy presence. Though I see Thee not, Thou hast
taught me to search for Thee. Though in infinite
distances Thou art enthroned, our humble earth
is Thy footstool. Though Thou dwellest afar, Thou
hast assured me that Thou wilt be near if I call
unto Thee in truth.

O keep Thou within my frail heart the thirst
to know Thee. May I never falter till I find the
living waters of Thy presence. Grant me the
strength to seek Thee with prayer and thanksgiving. Send me forth to search for Thee in all
Thy universe. Enhearten me with the hope that if
I call Thee, Thou wilt be near; if I seek Thee, I
shall find Thy presence.

Divine Source of light and truth, bless Thou my
blinded sight. Grant a vision of Thee to those who
yearn for Thy presence, so that familiar things may
be transfigured for us, that we hear the melody of
nature endlessly chanting of Thee, the silent speech
of day unto day, and behold the revelations of the
heavens declaring Thy glory. AMEN.

Wholeness of Character

Lord, who shall sojourn in Thy tabernacle? Who shall dwell upon Thy holy mountain? He that walketh uprightly, and worketh righteousness, and speaketh truth in his heart.

Now therefore fear the Lord, and serve Him in sincerity and in truth.

Psalm 15, 1–2; Joshua 24, 14.

No man's prayer is given hearing, unless when he raises his hands to heaven in prayer, he also raises his whole soul heavenward in his hands; for Scripture saith (Lam. 3, 40), "Let us lift up our heart with our hands unto God in the heavens".

Talmud (Taanit, 8a).

Every disciple whose inward thoughts do not correspond with his outward behavior is no true disciple of the sages.

Talmud (Yoma, 72b).

Our natural sympathy with our common human frailties often gives way when we find ourselves confronted by any form of treachery, hypocrisy and insincerity. When the false, the faithless, the insincere cross our path, seeking to deceive us, when we discover that the sentiments of their hearts are contrary to the language of their mouths, our soul is set ablaze with indignation.

And it is right that this should be so. For what is sincerity? It is nothing more nor less than wholeness of character. It implies absolute genuineness, free from the thinnest veneer of concealment. In our associations with men and women, we do right when we seek to be sure that they are genuine, wholesouled; that they mean what they say; that their actions are free from any cloak of pretence. At the heart of all of us lies the conviction that sincerity is not a special grace, a mere adornment of the soul, but that it enters into the very structure of character. Insincerity is the sure index of a double life, a shattered, disintegrated personality. There can be no honesty, no real truthfulness, unless there be sincerity in thought. Sincerity is not merely a virtue; it is the essence of all virtues. Only when our whole life is true and pure is sincerity possible.

O Lord my God, as I turn my thoughts to Thee and Thy great truths, I become conscious of the unity of life amidst all its diversities. By Thy grace it has been given me to see that Thy spirit pervades the entire realm of nature and every nook and corner of my own inner being. I yearn, O God, to become at one with Thee, to live in harmony with Thine immutable Law. Help me, O Father, I pray Thee, to attain unto wholeness of life. Create in me a pure heart, a heart that is spotless and clean, free from dross and counterfeit. May I ever be honest in word, in thought, in deed. Purify me, Thou who art the source of all purity, that I may be able to make sincerity the controlling influence in my life. O let Thy light and Thy truth ever lead me that through me others may rise to a deeper knowledge of Thy truth and all-encompassing love. Thou who desireth truth in the inward parts, teach me so to live that my inner life will need no concealment but will ever shine forth in radiant purity and nobility. AMEN.

The Just Life

Righteousness and justice are the foundation of His throne.

Justice, justice shalt thou follow, that thou mayest live, and inherit the land which the Lord thy God giveth thee.

Let justice well up as waters, and righteousness as a mighty stream.

Psalm 97, 2; Deut. 16, 20; Amos 5, 24.

These are the ordinances God spoke unto them, Whatever I do is done in justice. Was I to deviate from justice but once the world would cease to exist.

Midrash (Tanhuma, ed. Buber to Exod. 21, 1).

The world rests upon three things: upon truth, upon justice and upon peace. All these three are really one, for when justice is done, the truth becomes an actuality, peace a reality.

Talmud (Jerus. Taanith IV, 2).

God said unto Israel: Verily, My children, it is when you observe justice that I am most exalted.

Midrash (Deut. Rab. V, 7).

It is not a mere fancy of the human mind to compare justice to the scales of the balance that show the perfect poise. Even as the planets are held in their path by the power of attraction and repulsion perfectly balanced, so is this world of men saved from confusion and collapse by justice that holds in poise the balance of life. Justice defines the true relation of things. It is not the man-made enactment of legislatures; it is the law of God planted in the bosom of nature and rooted in the heart of man.

To tamper with justice is to create antagonism and strife. Justice is our friend, our ally, in all that makes for human happiness. It makes secure our life and property; it brings to us peace and joy and enlargement of soul. There can be no true happiness, there can be no true usefulness, without justice. All virtues, all graces, wait upon it. Justice is not the antithesis of love; it is love in action. It is truth at work. It is applied honesty. Unlike other virtues, it does not deal with the self; it represents our relation to our kind. Whether it be between man and man, or between men and men; whether it be between individuals or groups of individuals; justice seeks to maintain harmony and peaceful relations. How soon all wars would cease, all strife, all exploitation and oppression disappear, were justice permitted to exercise its divine function, to balance the forces of life!

My God and Father, Thou who rulest the world in wisdom and justice I lift my soul unto Thee in prayer and praise and thanksgiving. I praise Thee for the sense of justice which Thou hast implanted within me, and which ever seeks, though at times haltingly and gropingly, to express itself in the daily relations of life. I thank Thee for the inspired teachers of my people who have taught that Thou dost maintain the eternal order of the universe and that we are co-workers with Thee in the creation of order and peace in the world of human kind.

Be with me, O God, as I strive to do Thy will. Teach me to see that the men and women about me are my brothers and sisters, that when I hurt the least of them, I disturb the moral order of this world. Fill me with an ardent love for all Thy creatures that I may never be tempted to wrong them, to exploit their labor or services, or to take advantage of anyone's weakness or want or ignorance.

Kindle in me a passion for doing only that which is just and honorable. Grant me the vision to see that only justice can endure, and that only in being just to all others can I make my life acceptable to Thee. Help me by my thoughts and deeds to hasten the day when wrong and violence shall cease and justice be established in all the affairs of men. AMEN.

Ignorance and Evil

That the soul be without knowledge is not good. Happy is the man whom Thou instructest, O Lord, and teachest out of Thy law; that Thou mayest give him rest from the days of evil.

This is the covenant that I will make with the house of Israel after those days, saith the Lord, I will put My law in their inward parts, and in their heart will I write it; for they shall all know Me, from the least of them unto the greatest of them, saith the Lord.

Proverbs 19, 2; Psalm 94, 12, 13; Jer. 31, 33, 34.

All the great evils which men cause to each other originate in ignorance, which is absence of wisdom. A blind man, for example, who has no guide, stumbles constantly, because he cannot see, and causes injury to others. In the same manner, various classes of men, each man in proportion to his ignorance, bring great evils upon themselves and upon other individual members of the species.

The knowledge of truth removes hatred and quarrels and prevents mutual injuries.

Maimonides, 12th Century (Guide, Part III, Chap. XI, trans. Friedlander).

Ignorance contributes to every type of evil. Although there are some who know the good but consciously choose evil, yet most of us fall into the captivity of sin merely through lack of knowledge. We sin against our health through ignorance of physical laws; we sin against society through blindness to the laws of social progress; we sin against our heavenly Father by failing to understand what He doth require of us.

"An ignorant man," say the Rabbis, "cannot be truly righteous." He who does not know his own nature or the nature of his fellow men, blunders into errors and injustice. The first step out of evil must be made in the direction of enlightenment. We must seek to discover the true motives of our fellow men, so as never to sin by misjudging them. We must learn the laws of our souls so as to live lives worthy of our innate divinity. We must meditate on God's laws, so as to make our own will harmonize with His.

When we glimpse even a vestige of God's purposes, then we learn how to receive our good fortune in gratitude, and never fall into the sin of vainglory; we accept pain in patience, avoiding the iniquities of bitterness and rebellion. As knowledge of the laws of science will abolish many physical ills, so knowledge of the laws of God will cure men of anger, selfishness and hatred. The age of universal peace and brotherhood will be born of a deepened understanding—'the earth shall be filled with the knowledge of God, as the waters cover the sea.'

Lord, God of Knowledge, no human thought is hidden from Thee. Man's pretensions to knowledge are vain, and his boasted wisdom is empty in the light of Thine omniscience.

O Father, I have foolishly confounded good and evil, the true and the false; and now in my darkness I turn my thoughts to Thee in whom there is no ignorance and no evil. Send forth Thy light that it may lead me. Grant that Thy truth may have free access to my mind. Deepen within me the love of knowledge. Enlighten me with true understanding that I may check evils by discovering their source.

Teach me to understand Thy beneficence that I may never rebel against Thy word. Make me conscious of the brotherhood of all Thy children that I may be delivered from the sin of hatred. Grant me a glimpse of Thy gracious purposes that I may never despair. O lead me from the knowledge of Thy will to a fuller knowledge of Thee, Thou ultimate reality, infinite and eternal. AMEN.

Conciliation

A soft answer turneth away wrath, but a grievous word stirreth up anger.

Leave off contention before the quarrel break out.

Do good, seek peace and pursue it.

Proverbs 15, 1; 17, 14; Psalm 34, 14.

The followers of the sages augment peace in the world.

Talmud (Beracot, 64a).

One of the things having fruitage both in this world and in the hereafter is the act of conciliating men with one another.

Talmud (Peah, I).

In a world abounding in diversities of temperaments, environments and experiences, spontaneous harmony between individuals and nations is rare. The temptation to quarrel is inevitable. Unless there be conciliation there can be no peace.

The longer a contention has lasted the harder does yielding become, hence the Scripture bids us "leave off contention *before* the quarrel break out." The best time for yielding is before the strife has made headway. In warfare whether between individuals or between nations, the original grievance is soon obscured amid the growing accumulation of incriminations and recriminations, retaliations and reprisals. The fire of contention feeds upon itself until it is beyond control. We must conciliate at the outset before conciliation grows too difficult. Too seldom do we reflect that if yielding be disagreeable for us, it is no less disagreeable for others.

Another obstacle to peace is the confusion of it with fear. We are readily deluded into the assumption that yielding is cowardice. Sometimes indeed men do yield because of cowardice; but more frequently it is because of cowardice that they refuse to yield; for what form of cowardice is more prevalent than the fear of being thought a coward! Let us yield for the sake of peace. There will then be no occasion to yield because of fear.

There are, of course, fundamental convictions in religion and morals upon which there may be no yielding. But often, when we assert that we are battling for our principles, the searching of our hearts may reveal that not our principles but our vanities are the object of our contention.

When our holiest convictions are assailed, and there can be no yielding, there can still be a conciliation, namely the conciliation of suffering, the willingness to endure for the sake of peace. Suffering obviates strife and thus becomes conciliation at its noblest.

O Eternal One, who makest peace in Thy high places, send peace unto Thy children. Teach me to love peace and to seek to establish it. Strengthen me to forgive wrongdoing. Teach me to endure for the sake of Thy name. I contemplate the holy men and martyrs by whom the world has been glorified, and I pray that my life be touched by their influence. My personal prerogatives—how unimportant! Peace among men—how vastly important! Conciliation not from fear but in the fearless quest of peace, O make this my aim, Thou Eternal One, that peace may increase in the world and the choice fruits of peace be reaped by all Thy children. AMEN.

Out of the Depths

Out of the depths have I called unto Thee, O Lord. Lord hearken to my voice; let Thine ears be attentive to the voice of my supplication. My soul waiteth for the Lord, more than watchmen for the morning; yea, more than watchmen for the morning.

Psalm 130, 1–6.

Repentance waiteth patiently at all times for the sons of men. When can a man be purified of iniquity? When he returneth to the King on High, and uttereth prayer from the depths of his heart, as Scripture saith: Out of the depths I call unto Thee.

Book of Splendor (Zohar), 13th Century (III, 69b).

Though sages have taught men not to judge each other harshly, to be tolerant of each other, yet all men know well that the lesson has remained unlearned. All men have felt the pain of the world's scorn, for there is no man that sinneth not. The world, ready with its praise for success, pours out its merciless rebuke upon the unfortunate. Few men receive human pity for their iniquities.

God has no contempt for human weakness. To His endless might, even the greatest are weak. He looks upon all men alike in lovingkindness, even as a father pitieth his children. Men judge by the outward sight, the Lord judges the heart. He pities weakness, He is aware of all hidden temptations, and He forgives sin, re-creating the broken man, granting a new heart and a clean soul.

When man has sinned grievously, when he is rejected of his fellowmen, and despised in his own heart, let him approach God humbly and reverently, but without fear. God is near to the humble. His mercies endure for ever.

Hear my voice when I call unto Thee, O God of righteousness. Men have looked upon my transgressions; they have mocked me. Out of the depths I lift up mine eyes to Thine eternal hills and call in trembling upon Thy name.

Men may recall all my failings, and recount to each other all my shortcomings. Yet I shall not heed the tongues of men, if I can but escape into the awesome silence of Thy presence. If Thou shouldst ever mark against me my transgressions I could never stand before Thee. But with Thee is forgiveness. In Thine eternal mercy, Thou pitiest my weakness and even my faintest strivings after Thee, Thou rememberest in love.

Redeem me, O Lord, by Thy help, for in Thee alone do I trust. Create me anew by Thy word. Let there be light in my darkness. Be Thou near to me and teach me to call upon Thee in truth. Amen.

God Our Refuge

Keep me, O God; for I have taken refuge in
Thee.
God is our refuge and our strength,
A very present help in trouble.
Therefore will we not fear, though the earth do
change,
And though the mountains be moved into the heart
of the seas;
Blessed is the man that trusteth in the Lord, and
whose trust the Lord is.

Psalms 16, 1; 46, 2–3; Jeremiah 17, 7.

The noblest fruit of the tree of prayer is communion with God, which, when a man partaketh
of it, bringeth life eternal. Such a soul will not
worry over the misfortunes of the time; it will never
cease to bear the noblest of fruits; fellowship with
God, and life in the radiance of Divine Glory.

*Isaac Arama, 15th Century (Adapted from
Akeda, LVIII, P. 13b).*

We can not maintain for ever the valor of our
hopefulness. Some day, the sun suddenly becomes
overcast, the winds rise ominously. The tempest of
trouble bursts in full fury over the ship of life, and
all of our fond hopes for a peaceful voyage seem to
have vanished for ever. No heart can be made
proof against storms. Misery and disappointments

come to every man. On those dark days, the success upon which we have proudly relied seems to be trivial, and even our smallest failures seem to grow to disastrous size.

When despair enters the heart, no human aid can wholly expel it. The sun of life has become darkened, what can restore the light? Our vision is now blinded. We are afraid and impatient. No argument, no human encouragement will avail. We need a refuge, a quiet land-locked harbor, where, in the serene presence of Infinity, we can find rest.

To rest in the Lord, we must first earnestly seek the eternal Refuge. The Lord of Peace has, indeed, the blessing of peace for us, but He does not thrust upon us unsought comfort. His words will renew hope, but we must first listen eagerly before He speaks to us. We must yearn for Him, and turn to Him and seek Him in times of despair. Having found Him we will have found peace; and having rested in the peace of His presence, we shall have found serenity of mind and hope renewed.

Heavenly Father I seek refuge in Thee. I seek rest and peace for I am tossed by storms. I seek strength and courage, for I have lost hope. Days have come when only Thou canst help me. Be Thou with me when my days darken; when my toil seems vain, and my friends far away; when I am alone and have none but Thee.

I remember Thy words of old: "Seek Me and live." Keep within me, O my Father, the thirst to know Thee, that I may ever seek Thee. Sorrow and disappointments have humbled me. O be Thou near to the broken and contrite heart. I search for Thee; bring me into Thy presence. None can aid but Thee; send me Thy help. I trust in Thee for ever. AMEN.

God Is Near

Thou art nigh, O Lord, and all Thy command-
    ments are truth.
For thus saith the High and Lofty One,
That inhabiteth eternity, whose name is holy;
I dwell in the high and lofty place,
With him also that is of a contrite and humble
    spirit,
To revive the spirit of the humble, and to revive the
    spirit of the contrite ones.
The Lord is nigh to all that call upon Him; to all
    that call upon Him in truth.
        Psalm 119, 151; Isaiah 57, 14; Psalm 145, 18.

Fain would my heart come nigh
To Thee, O God on high,
But evil thoughts have led me astray
    From the pure path of righteous government.
Guide Thou me back into Thy holy way,
    And count me not as one impenitent.
O would that I might be
A servant unto Thee,
    Thou God by all adored!
Then, though by friends outcast,
Thy hand would hold me fast,
    And draw me near to Thee, my King and
    Lord.
        *Jehuda Halevi, 11th–12th Century (transl. by
        Alice Lucas).*

*Reprinted by permission of the Macmillan Co., from *The
Jewish Year* by Alice Lucas.

The very thought of the greatness of God, leads us at times to think of Him as dwelling far away. He is too great, we think, to concern Himself with little things, with unimportant man, with the trivial experiences of every day. Yet in truth it is the greatness of God which makes Him near unto us. For just as nothing is too difficult for His power, so nothing is too small for His omniscience and His love. His mercy shines into the farthest corners of the universe. He 'giveth food to the young ravens which cry'; He is near to the needy and the lowly. It was not in the storm or in the earthquake that Elijah found God, but in the still small voice. God is everywhere, far and near, in the infinities of the universe and in the chambers of the heart; in the mighty events which astound us, and in the song of a bird, the beauty of a flower and the smile of a child. His spirit is in the mission of a prophet and in the glory of a hero, and also in the love, service, joy and gratitude of humble men and women. Neither time nor distance limit God's love and help.

God is near when we bring Him near; He is far when we depart from Him. When we shout down the voice of duty, when we disregard God's law, when we shut our hearts to Him, then He seems to be far away, 'high and lofty, inhabiting eternity.' But when we seek Him, when His words are in our heart, and we meditate on them day and night, then 'God is nigh to those who call upon Him, who call upon Him in truth.'

O Infinite Lord, the heavens and the earth cannot contain Thee, much less the temples which men build. Thy being is timeless. What vision can the brief moment of the life of men give them of Thy reality. Yet in Thy majestic love Thou dost approach them, and in Thy mercy dost Thou lift up Thy countenance to illumine the places where they assemble to praise Thy name. Whenever Thy children call upon Thee, Thou revealest Thy presence.

Merciful Father, keep me near unto Thee. Thou art ever by my side, but I, alas, often flee from Thy presence. O let not the cloud of my mortal weakness, my selfishness and my discord shut out Thy light from me. Be Thou with me in all my undertakings. Keep me conscious of Thee, so that, when temptation comes, I may remain firm, when danger threatens, I may not lose heart, and when I walk through the valley of the shadow, I shall not fear, for Thou art with me. AMEN.

God's Love

For as the heaven is high above the earth, so great is His mercy toward them that fear Him. As far as the east is from the west, so far hath He removed our transgressions from us. Like as a father hath compassion upon his children, so hath the Lord compassion upon them that fear Him. For He knoweth our frame; He remembereth that we are dust.

For the Lord is righteous, He loveth righteousness.
O ye that love the Lord, hate evil.
And thou shalt love the Lord thy God with all thy heart, and with all thy soul and with all thy might.

Psalms 103, 11–14; 11, 7; 97, 10;
Deut. 6, 5.

When all within is dark,
    And former friends misprise;
From them I turn to Thee,
    And find love in Thine eyes.

When all within is dark,
    And I my soul despise;
From me I turn to Thee,
    And find love in Thine eyes.

When all Thy face is dark,
    And Thy just angers rise;
From Thee I turn to Thee,
    And find love in Thine eyes.

Solomon ibn Gabirol, 11th Century (Adapted
by I. A.).

Only an infinite love, lavishly generous and ever-true, can melt away the barriers dividing human hearts. Our blindness and our selfishness drive us far apart. How isolated we really are! How pitiful is our caution in our relations to one another! We are so hopelessly enmeshed in the net of personal interests, that we well may wonder, whence can come our help? We cannot rely upon the policies of worldly wisdom to bring us peace. We need a deliverance, a new vision, a glimpse of God's love, merciful and endless, patient and of infinite loving-kindness. When once we grow aware of the bound-less love we are daily receiving, our rancor will vanish, and we will learn to bestow generously the love which we abundantly receive. God's love is shining through the world, conquering the hearts of men.

God's love brings us His mercy; He is just, but He is more than just. His justice establishes the world; His love blesses it continually. When we ask that God reward our toil, and crown our un-completed lives with immortality, we are invoking His justice; and yet we tremble at its coming when we realize the extent of our sin and wilful rebellion. Then, pleading like erring children, we turn to His love, knowing that He is our Father as well as our King.

From the quarrels of men, from our own dark impulses which give them birth, and even from the just decrees of God's own judgment, we turn to God's love, in the hope that it will awaken in us a response, our love for Him. In our souls, once they are awakened unto love, hatred cannot abide, and we learn to come from the fields of discord unto the Tabernacle of Peace.

Father, gracious and compassionate, who sendest Thy love unto thousands of generations, be Thou my help! I do not rely upon my merits, for then, in justice, Thou couldst reject me utterly. Let Thy blessings come unto me as an unearned gift from Thee, my Father. Let Thy compassion be manifest, so that when I err, I may receive mercy and when I am misjudged, I may forgive.

Draw me nigh unto Thee that I may love Thee, and from love of Thee rejoice in Thy service. Make Thou my heart the channel for the stream of Thy love, so that, having been sustained by Thy patience I may be patient; having received Thy bounty, I may be bountiful; and having been blessed by Thy love, I may obey Thy behest to love my neighbor as myself. May I walk in the paths of Thy lovingkindness, bearing no illwill, forgiving hatred, and growing like unto Thee, gracious and compassionate. AMEN.

God's Bounty

O Lord, Thou maintainest my lot. My lines are fallen unto me in pleasant places, yea, I have a goodly heritage. I have set the Lord always before me; surely He is at my right hand, I shall not be moved.

Psalm 16, 5–8.

As for the man who relies upon the Lord, no abundance of wealth will ever diminish his trust in God, for he does not rely upon his wealth. He considers it to be merely a security left with him, to be used in a definite manner, for specific purposes, and for a limited time. If his wealth remain with him, he will never become proud and forget his duty to those whom God commands him to befriend, nor will the man who trusts in God ever expect gratitude and praise for his good deeds. Rather will he confess his own gratitude to God who gave him all these opportunities for benevolence.

If his wealth depart from him, he will not worry, nor mourn over his loss, but will be just as thankful to God who took back the pledge, as he was grateful to Him when he gave it.

Bachya, "The Duties of the Heart," 11th Century
(Introd.)

He who is blind to God's beneficence, ever stumbles in the darkness of error. He is oblivious of God's generosity, and so arrives at cynical and hard conclusions. If he achieves wealth or power, he believes that he has achieved it unaided, and that therefore he may enjoy it alone. Being conscious of no gift from God, he rarely feels the impulse of graciousness towards God's children. But a vision of God's bounty soon illumines the dark places of life. Let man but see how abundant is God's goodness, and his soul will be filled with the light of genial kindness. He will discover that the motive law of life is not selfish grasping, but generous blessing. The warming sun, the fruitful rain, the abundant earth and the magic seed, are God's messengers, carrying His gifts to the children of man. The very will of man, his persistence of purpose, the energy to toil, all come unearned from the Beneficent One. Man indeed labors—that is his destiny, but without God's gifts, he would not have the power to work, nor would his work bring blessing.

Let man think of God's endless goodness and be aware of the constant debt he bears his heavenly Father. Let the words of the Psalmist be in his heart: "How can I repay unto the Lord all His bountiful dealings towards me?" Let him vow to pay back to God's children the gifts which he has received. "My vow will I pay in the presence of all the people."

Gracious Father, Source of all joy, Fountain of the living waters of strength, Thou showerest Thy blessings upon me without stint. My powers, my achievements, my good fortune, my happiness, all come from Thee. O God, I pray Thee, add to Thy blessings unto me the consciousness of Thy goodness. As Thou givest me health and strength, give me too the vision to see Thy constant kindness. May I never cease to be grateful unto Thee. May I see Thy hand in the moulding of my life, and ever thank Thee.

Grant that my gratitude express itself in helpfulness. Teach me to walk in Thy footsteps; to be generous, helpful and good, so that my heart may reflect Thine endless bounty. May I be Thy messenger of blessing, aiding the poor, helping the helpless, healing the sick at heart. So will men know me for Thy agent, and thank Thee for the blessings I bestow. AMEN.

Rejoice in the Lord

Shout unto the Lord, all the earth. Serve the Lord with gladness; come before His presence with singing. Know ye that the Lord, He is God; it is He that hath made us, and we are His, His people, and the flock of His pasture. The Lord is good; His mercy endureth for ever.

Psalm 100.

Know thou, that whenever there rises upon the heart of men a sudden joyous thought, or a feeling of happiness, or a sense of love for God's law and commandments, that very moment is auspicious for prayer; and a prayer then uttered will reach upward to the presence of the holy King of Kings.

Hirsch Kaidanover, 18th Century ("Righteous Measures," 71, 8).

It is natural for us to seek God in times of sorrow. When we are unhappy, we feel our loneliness and long for His comfort and sympathy. Nor do we yearn in vain, for He giveth strength to the weary, and courage to the despondent. Our first religious experience often comes as we grow aware of His hovering presence consoling us in sorrow.

Yet a faith based upon such experiences alone, is sombre and incomplete. God reveals Himself in many ways, and His nature appears different to us as the angle of our vision varies. So we should seek Him in all the changing experiences of our life. Joyous moments may just as well reveal God to us as hours of saddened loneliness. Deep happiness can make us peculiarly receptive to His word. Joy expands the heart, opens the doors of generosity, and arouses a sense of gratitude. Happiness can be an ideal pathway to God's throne. In time of rejoicing, therefore, the exulting spirit should strive upward. Our lips should learn not only prayers of resignation, but words of praise and songs of gladness. We have often prayed to Him with bruised spirits. Now let the voice of joy and salvation rise up to Him from the tents of His children.

Heavenly Father, the morning stars sing together, the heavens rejoice, the earth is glad, and the sons of men chant unto Thee a new song. Joy pervading all the earth comes as a blessed gift from Thee. Thou biddest the sun to beam over the smiling earth and Thou lightest up my heart with gladness. Whenever my soul rejoices may I learn to feel my kinship with all Thy natural servants and to grow aware of Thy benign grace flowing within me.

Admit me into Thy presence in time of joy,

O heavenly Father, lest my laughter become law-less, my happiness unruly and my heart estranged from Thee. I seek Thee that my joys may be hallowed with Thee, that my happiness be deep-ened, that I join the chorus of the universe, lands and oceans, the stars and infinite space in joyous adoration. AMEN.

Reliance

Say among the nations: 'The Lord reigneth.'
The world also is established; it cannot be moved.
For ever, O Lord, Thy word standeth fast in
heaven.
Thy faithfulness is unto all generations.
They stand this day according to Thine ordinances; for all things are Thy servants.
Unless Thy law had been my delight, I should
have perished in mine affliction.

Psalms 96, 10; 119, 89–96.

How easily do we become panic stricken! When
some of the joys we seek elude us, when some
plans in which we had trusted end in failure, when
friends upon whom we have relied prove untrustworthy, then suddenly a sense of insecurity overpowers us. The whole world seems to grow
uncertain. Nothing tangible, nothing secure remains. We begin to see that wealth, no matter how
strongly entrenched and seemingly impregnable,
is suddenly swept away. Strong nations whose
might seemed endless, weaken and fall. Nothing
seems firm, nothing eternal. The rock upon which
we builded our house of life proves to be treacherous sand. We lean upon our house, it does not
stand.

Trust in the Lord at all times. The Lord is the

Rock of Ages. When the mountains move into the heart of the seas, He alone endures. Nations come into being; they plan and scheme to conquer the earth; the Lord bringeth to naught the councils of rulers; nations return into the darkness under His rebuke, but His purposes endure.

When under the stress of successive disappointments, human friendships seem to grow insecure, when life seems joyless and loveless, when to our harassed spirits it may seem that even father and mother have forsaken us, then this truth still remains: We can put our trust in His comfort and help. His mercy and His love endure for ever.

Eternal One, who changes not though all else vanish, from everlasting to everlasting, Thou art the same. We it is who vacillate and change. Like careless children we often forget Thee, and go astray after vain things that are of no avail. We put our reliance in the power of our arms, they weaken. We trust in our wealth, it disappears. We build upon might and power, they vanish. Then we sit upon the barren ground, amid the ruins of our world, desolate and forsaken.

O Eternal Father, I have gone astray. I have wandered away from the Fountain of living waters, into the desert of illusions. Bring me back to Thee. Teach me to trust in Thee alone, to rely upon Thy purposes, and to seek Thy love. Fortify me against the disappointments of the world. Put into my heart the unshakeable confidence, that though the mountains may depart and the hills be removed, Thy love and help will never depart from me and never wilt Thou annul Thy covenant of peace. AMEN.

Envy

Envy thou not the man of violence and choose none
of his ways.

My steps had well nigh slipped; for I was envious
at the arrogant.

A tranquil heart is the life of the flesh; but envy
is the rottenness of the bones.

For anger killeth the foolish man and envy slayeth
the silly one.

Proverbs 3, 31; Psalm 73, 2, 3; Proverbs 14, 30.

An envious eye, an evil mind and hatred of
fellow-creatures lead man to destruction.

Ethics of the Fathers (II, 16).

In the life to be, there is neither envy nor hatred,
nor contention, but the righteous rejoice in the
light of God's countenance.

Talmud (Beracot, 17a).

Jealousy is a disease of the spirit. It is the symp-
tom that something is wrong with the soul. Envy
is sin together with its punishment. It is an iniquity
which brings its own requital of misery. Like any
other sickness, envy can be cured only by the re-
moval of its causes. Excessive estimation of one's
self is the distortion from which envy arises. It is
bred from a wrong attitude of the mind. The mind
looks toward self when it ought to look toward
God.

Envy is always concerned with matters of inferior worth. One never envies in another, fine character, noble disposition, or unreserved consecration. The invariable objects of envy are wealth and fame, praise and comeliness, influence and position—in a word, material and perishable advantages. If the command to love God with heart and soul and might were literally obeyed, there would be no envy, for the destructive fire cannot rage without the fuel of low desires. When we long for Him with all our souls, we cease to long inordinately for those ephemeral advantages in which all envy centers.

Eternal One, Thou art my life, Thou art my health. My soul grows sick when removed from Thee. When separated from Thee, I fade and wither like the leaf separated from the stem. O let my love for Thee become perfected. So unstintedly may my heart be given unto Thee, that my mind and my hand may be given unreservedly to the duties that come from Thee. Be my soul so full of love that there will be no room for fretful jealousy, and my mind and hands so occupied with work that there will be no time for envy. Sweeten my life with Thy presence and calm me with Thy holiness. Purify me with Thy grace. For Thou art the purpose of my existence, Thou art my life's end and aim. AMEN.

Human Brotherhood

Love ye therefore the stranger, for ye were strangers in the land of Egypt.

And Solomon stood before the altar of the Lord in the presence of all the congregation of Israel and spread out his hands towards heaven and he said: Moreover concerning the stranger that is not of Thy people Israel, when he shall come out of a far country for Thy name's sake—for they shall hear of Thy great name and of Thy mighty hand, and of Thine outstretched arm—when he shall come and pray toward this house; hear Thou in heaven, Thy dwelling place, and do according to all that the stranger calleth to Thee for; that all people of the earth may know Thy name, to fear Thee, as doth Thy people Israel, and that they may know that Thy name is called upon this house which I have built.

Deut. 10, 19; I Kings 8, 41 ff.

'Thy priests are clad in righteousness.' This verse of the Psalms refers to righteous men of all nations. They are priests to the Holy One, blessed be He.

Midrash (Seder Elijah Zuta, XX, ed. Warsaw).

I call heaven and earth to witness that whether it be Gentile or Israelite, man or woman, slave or handmaid, the Divine Spirit rests upon all of them according to their deeds.

Midrash (Seder Elijah Rabba, ed. Friedmann, p. 48).

Judaism looks upon all human beings as children of one Father; thinks of them all as created in the image of God, and insists that a man is to be judged not by his religion, but by his action.

S. D. Luzzatto (Foundation of the Torah, p. 44).

Thou shalt love the stranger, is one of the noblest insistences of true religion. Man's untutored tendency is to love himself, and to consider his own conduct the proper rule of life. He is prone to feel contempt for strangers, and to despise strange ideas.

The faith of Israel began very early to combat the natural intolerance of men. The lesson of mutual tolerance was natural to it, for the religion of Israel grew up under stress. The sons of Jacob had been slaves under hard taskmasters. They had felt the bitter pain that is often the lot of the stranger. Thus they understood readily the behest of their leader: Love ye therefore the stranger, for strangers were ye in the land of Egypt.

Judaism developed the concept of God the Creator, the Universal Father to whom all men are children. Thence grew the conviction that the Lord is good to all and His tender mercies are over all His works. The royal builder of God's first sanctuary on Mt. Zion, dedicated the Temple with the prayer that God hearken to the supplication of the stranger who may come to seek His presence.

When, therefore, we consider ourselves the people chosen for God's service, we must accept our task in humility. It must not be a cause for haughty superiority. While we consider our faith to be true, we must not consider other faiths false. No bitterness should ever make us forget that, though men be strangers to each other, they are children to God.

O Exalted Power who inhabitest eternity, what can I say in Thy presence? Might is naught before Thee; pretensions are empty; human superiorities vain. When I forget Thee, I boast of my strength. I dream illusory dreams of greatness. I am childishly proud of myself, and scornful of my fellowmen. But in Thy presence and at Thy throne, all men stand in humble equality.

I thank Thee this day for the visions of ancient days; that Thou didst teach Thy seers to dream of all Thy children standing humbly in reverence before Thee, joined in mutual friendship. I thank Thee for all the ancient behests to love our neighbor as ourselves, and to love the stranger.

Heavenly King, Thou hast lovingkindness abundant for all Thy children. Grant unto me, I pray Thee, a measure of Thy goodness and of Thy tolerance; so that no hatred may ever blind me to another's godliness. May I be ever conscious of standing in Thy great Presence. O Source of all strength, grant me the power to endure adversity in patience, to meet harshness with gentleness, and to answer prejudice with serene tolerance, so that men may recognize that Thy Presence dwells with me, and through my humanity, learn of Thy divine mercy. AMEN.

Compensation

For they sow the wind and they shall reap the
    whirlwind.
The mind stayed on Thee, Thou keepest in perfect
    peace, because it trusteth in Thee.
Trust ye in the Lord for ever, for the Lord is God,
    an everlasting Rock.

Hosea 8, 7; Isaiah 26, 3–4.

The day is short, the work is great, the laborers
are slothful, but the reward is great and the Master
is urgent. It is not incumbent upon you to complete the work, but neither are you free to desist
from it altogether. Trustworthy is your Employer
to give you the reward of your labors.

Be as careful with what may seem to be a minor
duty, as with a grave one, as you can never know
the measure of reward allotted for duties performed.

Be not like servants who serve their master for
the sake of receiving a reward; be rather like
servants who serve their master without thinking
of the reward.

Ethics of the Fathers, II, 20, 21; I, 3.

The law of compensation is based on God's justice. "Shall not the Judge of all the earth do
justly?" "Far be it from Thee to slay the righteous
with the wicked, so that the righteous should be
as the wicked." We cannot believe that God, who

is just, will not distinguish in some way between those who have wilfully yielded to their lower instincts, and those who have disciplined their souls to live in toil and in righteousness.

Although the principle of compensation is fundamental to our faith, yet we can never calculate or predict the punishment or the reward of any man, for there are innumerable factors beyond our ken.

The mystery of reward and punishment remains hidden with God; but to us are revealed the duties of our life. He has given us many tasks, as difficult as they are exalted. We may never complete even one of them, but we cannot neglect them. Our reward is sure, although we cannot calculate it. Let us cease thinking of the wages of virtue, and devote ourselves to our work. Let us serve the Master without the constant dread of His punishment, and without endlessly estimating what reward we may receive for each act of righteousness. Let us trust in His mercy, and leave the reward to His beneficence. Let us never murmur at the prosperity of the apparently wicked; we cannot know all of their merits. Let us not despair at our own suffering; God has reasons beyond our finding out. It is for us to serve our Father, to trust in His justice and to hope for His mercy.

All-knowing Father, Ever-true, Thine omniscience and Thy justice are one! No human deed or thought is ever hidden from Thy sight. The labor of each of Thy creatures receives its reward. I trust in Thee at all times. Judge Thou the worth of my toil.

Heavenly Father, purify my heart. Inspire me to labor out of love for Thee, rather than for the gift of Thy blessings. Teach me to realize that while my reward will surely come, my duties are always before me. Urgent are the tasks Thou hast assigned to me, O Master, to do justice, causing hatred and persecution to cease; to love mercy, teaching forgiveness and benevolence; to walk humbly with Thee, reverently aware of Thy Holy Presence. Forgive me, I pray Thee, when I stray from Thee; and when I toil in Thy name, O establish Thou the works of my hands. AMEN.

Prayer for Others

Pray now unto the Lord our God for us.
Far be it from me that I should sin against the
  Lord in ceasing to pray for you.
And Moses cried unto the Lord, saying, 'Heal her
  now, O God, I beseech Thee.'
And Moses besought the Lord his God, and said:
  'Lord, why doth Thy wrath wax hot against
  Thy people?'

*Jeremiah 37, 3; I Sam. 12, 23; Numbers
12, 13; Exodus 32, 11.*

Whoso is able to pray for another but neglects
to do so is a sinner.

Talmud (Beracot 12b).

Our prayers should ever be the expression, not
alone of our yearning for communion with God,
but also of our deepest concern and love for our
neighbors and friends, for the whole world of
humankind. We ask, when we pray, for some
blessing, for some great gift from the boundless
store of God's bounty; but how soon would the
blessing, when granted to us, begin to pall and
end in joyless discontent, if any of our brothers
living by our side are pining and vainly struggling
for these same gifts with which we are happily

blessed! Can we be truly happy when God's own children are in misery and want? Yea, can we ignore the needs of our fellowmen and yet hope to receive an answer to our own petitions from Him whose love embraces all of His children?

It behooves us, therefore, to recall that we are not alone in this world, and that, when we breathe forth our petitions to God on high, we should reach out beyond ourselves and our own selfish interests. When our prayers are selfish, they lose their spiritual value and power. We come nearer to God, when we pray for the good of others. The noblest, because truest, kind of prayer is that which is offered in behalf of others. For such prayer marks our deepest realization that God is love. Such prayer reveals us to be one with those for whom we pray; and all spiritual union among the finite is a necessary condition as it is a clear intimation of our complete union with the Infinite.

Heavenly Father, Thou dost bid us love our neighbor as ourselves. I pray to Thee for many blessings, I seek mine own prosperity and health and joy at Thy hands. O grant me the love to seek with equal zeal the good of my fellowmen. Deepen my insight into the hearts of those around me. May I discover all that is precious within them and feel prompted to invoke upon them Thy blessing. Grant that I may look beneath and beyond all that is repelling and discern in others all that inspires love. As Thou art one and Thy name is one, do Thou unite Thy children. O bring us spiritually nearer to one another and thus eternally nearer to Thee. AMEN.

Righteousness

Seek good and not evil, that ye may live; and so the Lord, the God of hosts, will be with you as ye say.

Hate the evil and love the good, and establish justice in the gate.

Break Thou the power of the wicked; and as for the evil man, search out his wickedness, till none be found. Lord, Thou hast heard the desire of the humble. Thou wilt direct their heart, Thou wilt cause Thine ear to attend; to right the fatherless and the oppressed, that man who is of the earth may be terrible no more.

Amos 5, 14–15; Psalm 10, 15–18.

Right and justice are not simply matters for the state and the social order, but belong to God, who defends the cause of the helpless and the homeless, 'who executes the judgment of the fatherless and the widow,' who regardeth not persons, nor taketh bribes.' Iniquity is hateful to Him; it cannot be covered up by pious acts, nor be justified by good ends. 'Justice is God's.' Thus every violation of justice, whether from sordid self-seeking or from tender compassion, is a violation of God's cause; and every vindication of justice, every strengthening of the power of right in society is a triumph of God.

K. Kohler (Jewish Theology, pp. 120, 125).

When we consider that countless generations passed before the star of righteousness rose, then we can understand why so few as yet steer their lives and chart their courses by it. And yet righteousness is the inspiration of the vision and message of the prophets. They fearlessly identified the worship of God with the service of man; therein was revealed their marvelous courage. They insisted that God desires justice and not sacrifice, acts of mercy and not mere piety. Let not those whose hands are stained with blood come into His sanctuary. "Wash yourselves. Make yourselves clean. Put away the evil of your doings from before Mine eyes; cease to do evil; learn to do well; seek justice, relieve the oppressed, judge the fatherless, plead for the widow." Thus spoke the prophet Isaiah.

The world is still far from pursuing such principles. The faces of the poor are still ground into the dust. Injustice walks on the highway, and man can visit hunger and sorrow upon his fellowman.

But let none who is not clean of hands and pure of heart call himself by the name of the Most High God. He who would serve God must not only be guiltless of injustice; he must never regard wrong with complacency. His soul must flame with wrath at the tyrant. From his lips must burst the word of the Almighty God. His sword must leap from its scabbard to strike to earth the chains that bind men.

As children of Israel, the race from whose loins sprang the prophets, let us cherish the heritage of their spirit, and let us live by it.

Unto Thee do I turn, O God of Love, who dwellest with the humble and lowly. Thou desirest that man "walk uprightly, work righteousness and speak the truth in his own heart." Justice, and justice alone hast Thou asked him to pursue.

Grant me, I pray Thee, O Lord my God, a heart wide as the needs of men. I would not merely obey the law for the good of myself alone! Sympathy, only divine sympathy can teach me to stretch out a hand to the fallen, to heal the wounds inflicted by the cruelties of men. Teach my spirit to scorn whatever savors of tyranny and oppression. May I never grow cold and listless, or my ears grow dulled to the cry of distress. Grant that I may realize that I can serve Thee only by loving my fellowman as myself. Let me be rather of the humble than of the proud, of those who suffer than of those who crush; so that I may walk in Thy path and be at one with Thee, who lovest justice and establishest the world in righteousness. AMEN.

Hospitality

The stranger did not lodge in the street; my doors I opened to the roadside.

And lo! three men stood over against him; and when he saw them, he ran to meet them from the tent door, and bowed down to the earth and said: My lord, if now I have found favor in thy sight, pass not away, I pray thee, from thy servant. Let now a little water be fetched—and recline yourselves under the tree; after that ye shall pass on.

Job 31, 32; Genesis 18, 2–5.

Let the poor be members of thy household.

Ethics of the Fathers (I, 5).

A man's house should be open wide to the north, to the south, to the east, to the west—so that the poor should not be put to trouble in finding entrance.

Ethics of the Fathers of Rabbi Nathan, VII.

Hospitality is most blessed when brotherliness attends it. Our social divisions into classes did not exist in bygone centuries of Jewish life; the poorest sojourners were guests at the tables of the wealthy. Hospitality is at its fairest when the heart corresponds with the outward act. "Better is a dinner of herbs where love is, than a stalled ox and hatred therewith." Hospitality is at its noblest when it is the occasion not of mere indulgence but of lofty converse. Our sages have said: "If three have eaten at a table and conversed on sacred themes, they have, as it were, eaten at the table of the Most High."

Thoughts as well as persons can be objects of hospitality. As the individual whose home is open is more gracious than he whose doors are shut, so is the mind which is open to light from all directions more gracious than the mind that is barred and inaccessible. We must love the stranger for we were strangers in the land of Egypt. We must receive our fellowmen in kindliness for God is hospitable to us. The Psalmist said: "Thou preparest a table before me. Thou anointest my head with oil. My cup runneth over. I shall dwell in the house of the Lord." All of these treasured phrases are from the language of hospitality. For God is the host whose hospitality is at hand for our yearning hearts and souls.

O Heavenly Father, the heavens are Thy throne, the earth Thy footstool, all the world Thy house. I am but a stranger and sojourner before Thee. O receive me into Thy presence. Grant that by my daily acts of kindness, I may come to realize Thy boundless beneficence. May I perceive in every hospitality I confer or receive the image of that supreme hospitality whereby I feast at the table of life everlasting. May mine be a hospitality engaging the heart no less than the sense, not merely indulging the appetites but bringing light to the soul and transcending the unbrotherly lines of class separation; conscious that, before Thee, there is no division of higher and lower but only a brotherhood of Thy children, all alike bidden to share in Thy bounties unstinted. AMEN.

Our Enemies

I rejoiced not at the destruction of him that hated me, or exulted when evil found him.

If thine enemy be hungry, give him bread to eat, and if he be thirsty, give him water to drink.

Job 31, 29; Proverbs 25, 21.

Who is strong? He who converteth a foe into a friend.

Ethics of the Fathers of Rabbi Nathan (XXIII, 1).

Alas for him who saith: 'I have been humiliated, be my fellowman humiliated. I have been cursed, be he also cursed.' Let him remember when he humiliates and curses a human being, it is God's image that he humiliates and curses.

Midrash (Genesis R. XXIV, 7).

Our worst enemy is our self. Others may hate us but our own misleading phantasies and our ungoverned impulses are foes beside which all other foes are negligible. These baneful qualities within us are the cause of most of the hostilities that we suffer from others. We assume insults where insults were never intended and slights where slights were not dreamed of. Subsequent reconciliation and explanation reveal how unnecessary the suffering has been which we caused ourselves and others.

When a person is our enemy and dislikes or hates us, how shall we overcome his hatred? By retaliation? By inflicting reciprocal pain or injury? Surely not, but by substituting, so far as lies in our power, acts and attitudes that will help and gladden. No other antidote to hatred is conceivable. No other means of counteracting enmity are rational. To meet enmity with enmity is like fasting to overcome hunger, sprinkling oil to quench fire or pouring water to allay dampness. This is true of our national and racial hostilities as well as of our personal ones. When the misguided self of another cherishes hatred and our misguided self magnifies it, then naught can bring peace but patience and forgiveness. We must meet our fellow-man with the abundant lovingkindness which we ask of God.

Father Everlasting, who understandest the hearts of men, none is wholly righteous in Thy sight, yet Thou graciously pardonest Thy children, even when they rebel against Thee. Teach me, I pray Thee, to purify myself before I rebuke others. Open Thou mine eyes that I may be enlightened. Keep me from seeking foes where there are no foes, and give me the insight to seek within and rout my foes where foes really lurk. Take from my soul the indolence and vanity, the selfishness and thoughtlessness that bring me into ill favor with my fellowmen. Imbue me with that righteousness without which there can be no peace, that love without which there can be no harmony, that brotherhood without which there can be no concord. Not that I might love my enemies do I pray, but that I might through goodness transform them; nay, that I might regard none as my enemy. May there be granted me the wisdom to earn, through rectitude of my conduct, the love, regard and good favor of all whom my life may touch. AMEN.

God Our Sustainer

I lift up mine eyes unto the hills, from whence shall my help come? My help cometh from the Lord who made heaven and earth. He will not suffer thy foot to be moved. He that keepeth thee will not slumber; behold He that keepeth Israel doth neither slumber nor sleep.

The Lord is thy keeper; the Lord is thy shade upon thy right hand. The sun shall not smite thee by day, nor the moon by night.

The Lord shall keep thee from all evil; He shall keep thy soul.

The Lord shall guard thy going out and thy coming in, from this time forth and for ever.

Psalm 121.

Let man beware against going forth upon his journeyings alone. That is to say, let him obey the Divine Will so that he shall not go forth without the accompanying Presence of God—which will sustain him and deliver him in every hour of need.

Book of Splendor (Zohar), 13th Century (I, 459).

We cherish the hope of growing worthy of our innate godliness, and we know that the serious labor of noble living requires a spirit of sustained courage which no defeat can crush, and a high hopefulness which no success can corrupt. Such a sustained spirit is, alas, rare among us, for we are creatures of mood. Now we are elated at some trivial success, and now some chance event casts its shadows upon our hearts.

We forget to seek the Lord and His strength, for, in moments of minor achievement, we grow proudly self-sufficient. Our hand has wrought, our powers have achieved, our strength has accomplished. We need no help! Yet our self-reliance does not endure for, although it beseems us to stand proudly courageous as the children of the living God, the slightest failure drives us into dejection. Our hand seems weak; our powers puny, and our strength turned to water. An unbearable sense of our ineffectiveness crushes us to earth.

Thus driven by the stray winds of accident, from the proud harbor of exaltation to the rocks of despair, we turn from joy to sorrow, from sorrow to shortlived joy; we go from strength to weakness, and from weakness to illusions of strength. Left to our own resources, we endlessly waver, lacking the steadiness of aim, the firmness of purpose, which alone can make life nobly strong.

We need help from God. We need the consciousness of His unfailing presence, His immovable power, His everlasting help. Conscious of His sustaining strength, we remain moderate in our success knowing that He has aided us. We retain hope in time of failure, knowing that His hand can help. Never swerving from its course, guided by the star of its faith, our life pursues its steady progress.

Thou everlasting Help, be at my side. Thou hast ever been the help of our fathers throughout all generations. They trusted in Thee. Thus when hatred beset them, when their life seemed a futile struggle against implacable hostility, their consciousness of Thine everpresent aid saved them from despair.

O Eternal Power! Through all the changes of life, Thou dost not change. Teach me to look to Thee. Teach me to lean upon Thy strength. Let not pride corrupt me, nor weakness crush me. I lift up mine eyes to Thee. Thou wilt illumine my darkness. Sustain me; suffer not my foot to stumble. Make Thy Presence accompany me upon my way that I may walk firmly and confidently before Thee, toward the tasks which Thou hast set for me; leaning upon Thy help, fulfilling Thy purposes. AMEN.

Suffering

For whom the Lord loveth He correcteth, even as a father the son in whom he delighteth.

Thou didst loose my sackcloth, and gird me with gladness.

It is better to go to the house of mourning than to go to the house of feasting.

Proverbs 3, 12; Psalm 30, 12; Ecclesiastes 7, 2.

Said R. Elazar ben Jacob: "When sufferings come upon him, man must utter thanks to God, for suffering draws man near unto the Holy One, blessed be He. As it saith: "Whom the Lord loveth, He correcteth, even as a father correcteth the son in whom he delighteth." When griefs come upon a man, let him stand up and receive them.

Midrash (Tanhuma to Deut. 21, 10).

When suffering comes upon us, as it comes to all, we often fret despairingly and repine. We cannot understand why we should be made the apparent sport of misfortune and calamity. We wonder why tender affection should be created, only to be rudely broken; why agonizing pain should wreck our nerves and consume our flesh. In moments of great sorrow, the stricken heart is apt to exclaim: "Surely God does not care, or else why does he inflict upon me such cruel pain!"

Yet it is through struggle and sorrow that we learn to know more of the love and faithfulness of God than in any other way! We know only too well that sorrow often breaks the crust of a superficial life, uncovers its deepest realities. Through the dark cloud that envelops us, there breaks forth a new vision of the aim and purpose of our earthly existence. Not always on the heights, sometimes from the depths do we best see God. And seeing Him, we come to realize that our life is not a haphazard occurrence of chance events and circumstances, that a Divine hand and purpose are discernible in all that befalls us. Out of the dark passages of life, we emerge into the light of faith, purified in spirit, more keenly alert and responsive to the soft whisperings of the still small voice ever striving to speak to our hearts.

O Lord my God, I bow my head before Thee in humility and gratitude. When shadows enshroud me, when hardship and suffering invade the peacefulness of my life, I shall not lose faith and courage, for Thou art with me. Thy rod and Thy staff, they comfort me. When the clouds gather and the storm breaks, my heart will not faint and my steps will not falter, for I trust in Thee and cannot fear. Help me, O God, to be firm and steadfast, to fix my gaze upon Thee and Thy wisdom. When weary, fretful, and discouraged, teach me, O Father, to be still, bravely to face life, and confidently to look across the vale of shadows. Strengthen me, O God, that I may be able to bear pain, sickness, or danger, with faith and fortitude, with dignity and hope. AMEN.

Courageous Faith

Be as strong as a leopard, as swift as an eagle, as fleet as a stag, and as mighty as a lion in doing the will of thy Father in heaven.

Ethics of the Fathers, V, 23.

Like a swift moving fire which ceases not nor rests, until it has accomplished its purpose, so must man's energy be in the service of God.

Moses Hayyim Luzzatto, 1707–47
(Path of Upright, VII).

Venturesomeness is commonly associated with the career of the soldier, the explorer and the merchant. But there is also in religion a place for venturesomeness. There may be ventures for God and for the soul. The saints and the martyrs of history were God's adventurers.

The word "faith" in its worthy sense can mean naught else than an adventuring in God's name. Faith, properly understood, is not belief contrary to reason but conduct conformable to reason. In a world of impulses and passions, there is no conduct more venturesome and more holy than loyalty to the principles which our calmer moments have discerned. One who keeps his composure though a whole world rages, who is gracious even to injurers and detractors, who observes rigid honesty though destitution be risked, who cherishes his well reasoned convictions though a whole world persecutes, he who labors for peace amid a world at war, who speaks the truth though all others prevaricate, who is pure and candid though a whole world jeers—such a one is, of all adventurers, the bravest and the noblest.

Our sages say that we must be as swift as eagles and as strong as lions if we would serve our heavenly Father. All of our powers must unite at their best to succeed in life's greatest adventure, the pilgrimage to God's holy mountain where we may learn His ways. For we need a mighty faith to praise Him when we walk among men who mock at His word; we need endless trust to be patient in the vale of tears and we must find the strength to answer Him when He calls us to His work.

Happy is he who ventures thus. He shall dwell in the goodly tabernacles of the Lord of Hosts.

O Omnipotent Source of all Power, Thou hast put Thy spirit in Thy children and granted strength to the weak and courage to the despairing. With Thy help tyranny has been overthrown, peoples redeemed from bondage and the light of hope kept kindled in days of darkness. With Thee to aid, no task is too difficult; without Thee our strength fails and the slightest obstacles grow insurmountable.

Teach me, therefore, O Father, to seek Thee and Thy strength, that I may truly live. O strengthen me to venture everything for Thee. Fortify my soul to task itself to the utmost in order to enter Thy presence.

Teach me that the untried and untrod ways of life are not too perilous when it is Thy kingdom that I seek. O rebuke Thou my cowardice. Overcome my hesitation. Dispel my timidity. Spur my soul to venture all things for Thee. Amen.

Reverence

"And Jacob awaked out of his sleep, and he said: Surely the Lord is in this place; and I knew it not. And he was afraid, and said: How full of awe is this place; this is none other than the house of God, and this is the gate of heaven."

Genesis 28, 16–17.

To the reverent mind there is something profound and mysterious in everything that confronts our gaze. We look out upon the world of nature, and cannot but suspect a deep secret buried within its bosom. We behold man in the midst of his activities, and cannot but be impressed with the nobility of his soul, the sacredness of his life. We watch the elemental forces as they operate in nature and man, and cannot but stand in awe of their greatness and mystery. In fact, nature yields to us its deepest secrets, man discloses the supreme dignity of his life, only when we feel a deep reverence toward them.

And when we are thus actuated by the spirit of reverence, we are seldom content with idle contemplation. We seek to express it in forms of active service. We know that our reverence of God is true, when we yearn to serve Him, to learn His will and do it. We know that our reverence of nature is true, when we seek to understand her ways, to study her laws and obey them. And how can we prove true our reverence toward the mystery and greatness of the human soul, unless we strive to exalt and serve man, to recognize in every human relationship the sanctity of man's nature?

As an humble servant of Thy benign will, O God, I ask Thee to put into my heart the fear and love of Thee and to fill my soul with sincere reverence toward my fellowmen and all the sublime works of Thy creation. Quicken my conscience, I pray Thee, that I may desire more of the beauty of Thy holiness; that I may seek Thy will above all ambitions. Grant me the vision to see that it is Thy throbbing life that flows in every vein and spreads abroad in leaf and flower; that it is Thine own supernal glory that I behold in the beauty of earth and sky. Deepen my sense of unity, and increase my joy of brotherhood that I may learn to serve Thee by dispensing of my love and care to all Thy children. Hear my prayer, O Lord, who art my Strength and Redeemer. AMEN.

Holy Places

The Lord is in His holy temple;
Let all the earth keep silence before Him.
But as for me, in the abundance of Thy loving-
kindness will I come into Thy house.
I will bow down toward Thy holy temple in the
fear of Thee.
Surely the Lord is in this place and I knew it not.
The place whereon thou standest is holy ground.

Habakuk 2, 20; Psalm 5, 8; Gen. 28, 16;
Exodus 3, 5.

Whoso walketh in haughty pride repels the presence of God.

Talmud (Beracot 43b).

Whoever committeth sins in secret repels the
presence of God.

Talmud (Hag. 16a).

God's presence abideth not amidst indolence,
vexation, frivolity, levity, chatter or gossip but
amidst holy joy.

Talmud (Sabbath 30a).

When a man prayeth he must demean himself
as if the Divine Presence is before him.

Talmud (Sanhedrin 22a).

Whoso goeth from synagogue to school house
cometh face to face with God.

Talmud (Beracot 64a).

Any place which evokes ignoble motives loses whatever sacredness it may have possessed. If even a synagogue become the scene of prejudice, cynicism or animosity, its holiness becomes profaned. But any place which strengthens the better part of our nature, is holy. A workshop wherein one labors with enthusiasm and zeal or an open field where one ardently and lovingly raises sustenance from the earth or a market place in which ideals of brotherhood and good will are conceived and pursued can be holy places.

The sanctity of the places to which we come, depends, in no small measure, upon ourselves. No place can be holy to him who is unresponsive to noble appeals; while all the world is a sanctuary to the soul that is alive to all that is good, beautiful and true. And therefore, under normal conditions, home is of all places the holiest. It is a sign of some abnormality when home ceases to be one of the sanctuaries of our life. Any place where we have discerned some new beauty is holy. The place where we have transcended some mighty sorrow; the place where we have performed some noble act of self-renunciation; the place where we have zealously worked; the place where we have earnestly prayed; or the place where we have abandoned some injurious error and turned our face to the light, shines ever after with the beauty of holiness.

When, therefore, our synagogues, already blessed
with sacred memories, are filled with the voice of
earnest prayer and song, whenever the word of
God uttered within it enters into loyal hearts,
then the house of prayer becomes a true sanctuary,
and the temple built by the hands of men, becomes
God's dwelling place.

O Thou whom the seraphim declared thrice
holy, the whole universe is full of Thy glory.
Wherever Thou dost reveal Thyself is holy ground;
at Sinai in the desert, in the Temple where Thou
didst call unto Samuel. Wherever Thy name was
mentioned in reverence, Thou didst come and bless
with Thy holiness. Whenever we seek to turn from
Thee, the beauty of Thy holiness departs from us,
and even places dedicated to Thy worship become
profane.

I pray Thee, O Lord, keep me near to Thee,
lest the glory of my life depart. Quicken the foun-
tains of love and beauty within me that the place
whereon I stand may become unto me in fuller
measure, holy ground. Inspire me to be holy as
Thou art holy, to walk in Thy footsteps, practic-
ing lovingkindness and seeking peace and truth,
until humble places become glorified by Thy presence, my heart a fit dwelling place for Thee, and
all the world a Beth El, a House of God. AMEN.

The Presence of God

Whither shall I go from Thy spirit? or whither shall I flee from Thy presence?

If I ascend up into heaven, Thou art there; if I make my bed in the nether world, behold, Thou art there. If I take the wings of the morning, and dwell in the uttermost parts of the sea; even there would Thy hand lead me, and Thy right hand would hold me. And if I say: 'Surely the darkness shall envelop me, and the light about me shall be night'; even the darkness is not too dark for Thee, but the night shineth as the day; the darkness is even as the light.

Seek ye the Lord while He may be found, call ye upon Him while He is near.

Psalm 139, 7–12; Isaiah 55, 6.

The eye of faith is blessed with the vision to discern God not alone in the heavens above and the earth below, but in every circumstance and mood of life. Above nature is its Creator. We are not mere wheels in a machine. The affairs of this world are governed by a guiding thought and power. Whether we live in joy or sorrow, in peace or in strife, in rest or in weariness, all that we behold is animated and beautified by the spirit of the living God. His unseen presence surrounds us and enters into our souls. He is near us, giving us strength even though we do not feel it, sending us help even though we do not know it. Noiselessly His manifold blessings steal into our lives. He is always close to this mysterious, bewildering life of ours, for ever seeking to fill us with a knowledge of Himself, for ever working upon our souls to make them pure and strong, good and true.

Not alone in set hours of devotion is God present, but whenever and wherever the soul is ready to receive Him. All things reveal God; all worthy efforts disclose His presence. All duties, the most menial of occupations, are expressions of His spirit. Nothing that we do is ever secular, if we but know how to make our tasks divine. Our daily duties can become channels of His truth and love. For God is everywhere, in the song of the bird and in the beauty of the rose, in the smile of the child and in the wrath of the seer, yea, in the love and service of the humblest man and woman. "The Lord is nigh unto all that call upon Him, to all that call upon Him in truth."

Almighty God and Father, Thou keepest constant guard and watch over all Thy people. Thou art at my right hand, and I know that I cannot be moved. I give Thee heartfelt thanks, O Lord, for the enduring faith, the common hope and purpose, of Thy people Israel. May Thy spirit ever be with me, to broaden and deepen my life. When doubt assails me, give me, I beseech Thee, such realization of Thy presence as will save me from confusion and distrust. Thou hast implanted within my heart an inextinguishable longing for Thee. Reveal Thyself more clearly to my yearning heart, and send me forth amid the cares and trials of this world sustained by the consciousness of companionship with Thee. Help me to behold Thee in all familiar experiences of life. May the sense of Thy nearness put to flight the petty cares and fears that so often consume the joy and nobleness of life. Open mine eyes, I pray Thee, that I may see Thine image in the souls of my fellow beings; and teach me so to serve, that I may confirm my brotherhood with them and my joyous union with Thee. AMEN.

Vision and Hope

All the world shall come to serve Thee
And bless Thy glorious Name,
And Thy righteousness triumphant
    The islands shall acclaim.
And the people shall go seeking
    Who knew Thee not before,
And the ends of the earth shall praise Thee,
    And tell Thy greatness o'er.

They shall build for Thee their altars,
    Their idols overthrown,
And their graven gods shall shame them,
    As they turn to Thee alone.
They shall worship Thee at sunrise
And feel Thy kingdom's might,
And impart their understanding
To those astray in night.

They shall testify Thy greatness,
And of Thy power speak,
And extol Thee, shrined, uplifted
Beyond man's highest peak.
And with reverential homage,
Of love and wonder born,
With the ruler's crown of beauty
Thy head they shall adorn.

With the coming of Thy kingdom
The hills shall break into song,
And the islands laugh exultant
That they to God belong.
And all their congregations
So loud Thy praise shall sing,
That the uttermost peoples, hearing,
Shall hail Thee crowned King.

The tenacity of our courage depends upon our larger ideals. Whenever we despair of humanity, we despair of ourselves. Whenever we are poisoned by the thought that mankind labors in vain, our own labor inevitably grows weak and dispirited. Our power to continue even our humblest tasks is rooted deeper than we realize in the soil of our own dreams of God's kingdom on earth.

The prophets and the psalmists of Israel encouraged the humble with visions of glory. When men stumbled in the darkness of grief, they bade them 'rise, shine with the glory of God,' assuring them that 'nations would walk by their light.' When men were saddened and embittered, the psalmist cried out: 'Sing unto the Lord a new song,' for the time would surely come when all the nations of the earth would shout for joy unto the Lord.

Without vision we perish. To endure the present, we must dream of the future. We cannot live from day to day without the hope that day is added unto day, and that even the humblest of our achievements count in the total reckoning. Our struggle assumes a new value and our labor a new dignity if we believe that our every action is treasured by our Father, and by His aid, brings nearer the day when war shall cease. How very good it is to seek the Lord when we know that every new vision of Him becomes immortal and that, by our growing knowledge of Him, we are hastening the day when all the earth shall be filled with the knowledge of God as the waters cover the sea.

O Eternal One, my days are measured by Thine infinity, and are but a passing breath. The thought of Thy greatness terrifies me, and in my weakness, I foolishly imagine that Thou dost not regard me, that my efforts are vain and my achievements lost as a voice in the wind. Grant me courage, O Father. Send me the assurance that as Thy words are eternal, so dost Thou crown my strivings and dreams with immortality; that no true hope ever perishes and no high vision fades; that Thou preservest all my aspirations so that their total may add to the merit of Thy children and brighten Thine image within them.

I need Thy help, O God, for I am mortal and weak. Selfishness, blindness and rage often control me, and I delay Thy kingdom as frequently as I hasten it. O illumine my blindness, and enlarge my vision; pardon mine anger and increase my serenity; forgive mine iniquities and treasure my goodness, so that, in Thine own time, I may join with all men in acknowledging Thee and live in Thy light, throughout all my days. AMEN.

Duty

Show me Thy ways, O Lord; teach me Thy paths.

Guide me in Thy truth, and teach me; for Thou art the God of my salvation; for Thee do I wait all the day.

Psalm 25, 4–5.

The voice of duty must be, for every individual, the voice of God. Duty may be humble but it is never trivial. Our duty signifies our place in the universe, for the laws of the universe are service, justice and love.

What is our duty? An abstract definition of duty is difficult, yet, in our practical life, there are very few doubts that duty presents! The very next thing to do, the very next step to take is always certain. We are like a man with a lantern on a dark road. The lantern shows its bearer only the first step ahead. But that suffices. Let the first step be taken and the next step will be illumined and then the next step and thus to the journey's end.

Duty is the foundation of all that is excellent in human existence. It is the basis of service toward others and of benefit for one's self. Without duty there can be neither sustenance nor health, neither justice nor friendship, neither knowledge nor peace. How poise, character and happiness disintegrate when duty is ignored! The commandments of God form a system of duties, duties to our fellowmen, to our souls, and to God, our Father. Without them there is neither happiness nor peace.

Thou art calling me, Lord. Out of eternity Thou art summoning me to become a sharer in Thy kingdom of order and beauty. By the bridge of duty I may pass from chaos to creation.

Grant, I beseech Thee, that my duties may evoke my zealous devotion. When Thou callest me may I give eager answer to Thy summons: Speak, Lord, Thy servant heareth Thee. Lead me along the paths of duty for they are the paths of peace. O enable Thou me so to acquit myself that there may come unto me the serenity and deep contentment which duty alone conferreth and which only they can find who heed Thy blessed call. AMEN.

Accepting the Burden

It is good that a man should quietly wait
For the salvation of the Lord.
It is good for a man that he bear
The yoke in his youth.
Before I was afflicted I did err; but now I ob-
serve Thy word. It is good for me that I have
been afflicted in order that I might learn Thy
statutes.

Lamentations 3, 26, 27; Psalm 119, 67, 71.

When mankind languisheth in pain let no man
say I shall return unto mine own household, eat
and drink and be at peace! Nay, each man must
be willing to suffer with his fellowmen. He who
shares the afflictions of others will merit to behold
the comforting of humanity.

Talmud (Taanith 11a).

The psalmist recalls the sombre days of his
affliction, the sudden disaster, the dazed heart
heavy with grief, then the gradual healing of the
wounded spirit, the chastened soul, the deepened
understanding, and the blessed sense of God's comfort and mercy. All this he recalls and praises the
Lord: 'It is good that Thou hast afflicted me, for
thus have I learned Thy statutes.'

When we live at ease we sail carelessly over the surface of life unaware of its deeper undercurrents. Then calamity overtakes us, and, in the struggle with the waves, we learn how precious is life, how deep is pain, how boundless our gratitude to our Deliverer and Preserver. God brings us to the very gates of death, in order that we may learn, manfully, how to choose life.

It is not only our own affliction which brings us blessing. The sufferings of our fellowmen often redound to our benefit. From their tragedies we learn how to avoid misfortune. Even the material comforts of our life are largely due to suffering of those who lived before us. The houses in which we live, the fuel we burn, the streets we traverse, all have a history of toil, suffering, danger, and even death. The musician who delights us with his art, the teacher who brings light to our minds, the physician who rescues us from pain, all have endured years of self-denial, toil and trouble. We live by the sufferings of the mother who gave birth to us and the parents who reared us. The beautiful lives which inspire us have been wrought in the furnace of affliction. The call comes to all of us to bless as we have been blessed; to accept our share of this interblend of pain and benefit. We who profit by the vast linkage of human woe and weal cannot refuse the burden of pain. We must patiently accept the daily restraints of conscience, and walk the arduous way of virtue. Perhaps others may profit by our strivings and find in our humble lives a blessing.

In Thy mercy, O God of Love, Thou causest light to shine in hours of darkness. Teach me, O Lord, to trust in Thy love, to accept with patience the grief Thou sendest. Grant me the hope that I may behold my afflictions as a means of my spirit's enlightenment. Open mine eyes to see that none liveth to himself alone; that innumerable are the strands binding each to each. May my sorrow be hallowed and solaced by the thought that as no man liveth for himself alone, no man suffereth for himself alone; that all that suffering createth, whether of beauty within us or of achievement for the good of others, belongeth not to one but to all. Our sufferings can become highways to the goals of love. Lead us therefore in the paths of love that our every sorrow may be endured for Thy name's sake, so that even the valley of the shadow may become a pathway where I may walk with Thee. AMEN.

God Our Eternal Home

Lord, Thou hast been our dwelling place in all generations.

Psalm 90.

Home offers shelter and peace. Home is the sanctuary within which life's fiercest struggles abate. There, more than anywhere else, individuality has free play. Outside of the home our wishes must be curbed, our tastes overriden, our convenience ignored; but in the home, the multitude is excluded, and our individuality reassumes its dignity.

God is our eternal home because, unlike finite man who ignores much and heeds little, the Infinite ignoreth naught and heedeth all. Our individuality is precious and indispensable unto Him.

Unto the Divine Father naught is outcast, naught strange, naught negligible. The weakest and the obscurest are significant unto Him. The psalmist has said: "We are the people of His pasture and the flock of His hand." "Like as a father pitieth his children, so the Lord pitieth them that reverence Him." "Though father and mother forsake me, the Lord will take me up."

Closely linked with our consciousness of every individual's worth is our consciousness of immortality. A heightened sense of the preciousness of the individual to God brings with it a clearer intimation that the soul is deathless. If we are cherished children to our Father, then are we immortal. The moment we sense God as our home, we know Him to be our eternal home.

O Thou whose mercies are infinite, open mine eyes to the beauty and worth of every human soul. Heal my blindness. Enable me to peer beneath the outward appearance to the realities within. Give me that grace of mind and nobility of character that can penetrate beneath all that is unpleasant and forbidding in my fellowmen and let me behold that precious core in individuality whereby humanity becomes divine and all hearts are linked together because linked unto Thee.

Yea, in Thee we are at home, Eternal One, and only in Thee. Though we seem homeless amid life's storms, Thou alone art acquainted with all our ways. Thou wilt not abandon our soul to the grave, Thou wilt show us the path of life. AMEN.

Humility

Now the man Moses was very meek, above all men that were upon the face of the earth.

When pride cometh, then cometh shame; but with the lowly is wisdom.

Thus saith the Lord: Let not the wise man glory in his wisdom, neither let the mighty man glory in his might, let not the rich man glory in his riches; but let him that glorieth glory in this, that he understandeth, and knoweth Me, that I am the Lord who exerciseth mercy, justice and righteousness in the earth; for in these things I delight, saith the Lord.

Numbers 12, 3; Proverbs 11, 2; Jeremiah 9, 22–23.

It is better for a man to be told, 'Arise, ascend from thy lowly station,' than to be told, 'Descend from thy place of pride.'

Midrash (Exodus 4, 1).

Thus Scripture teaches us that he who is humble brings God's presence close unto earth to dwell among men.

Mekilta to Jethro.

Humility is the noblest virtue of a religious life. It is the key that unlocks the precious treasures of spiritual understanding. When we are self-willed and arrogant, when we assume the haughty mood, the most obvious facts of our existence become shrouded in obscurity. Truth, ever ready to yield itself to the inquiring mind, shrinks from the withering look of the proud. Only when we feel profoundly humble, only when we are conscious of our own weakness, of the uncertainty of our own steps, do we feel impelled to struggle for knowledge, for light and guidance; and only then can we hope to obtain enlightenment.

It is the sense of dependence, which is the very essence of humility, that fills us also with a desire to search for the source of all truth and wisdom, the great Rock in whose shadow we may ever find comfort and strength as we wander through the weary land. When we seek Him we find life a delight. A vision of His greatness and His glory breaks upon us like the radiant morning dawn, and, with wholeness of heart and complete self-surrender, we adore and glorify His name.

O Lord, my God, King of the universe, Father of all men, Thou art great, and Thy name is exalted above all. All that I am and all that I may yet be, come from Thine aid. Without Thy guiding hand and sustaining power, of what avail would my efforts be!

With my head bowed in humility, and my lips attuned to praise, I ask Thy help. Give me, I pray Thee, a wise and constant heart that I may never be moved to haughtiness of spirit and self-pride. Imbue me with the consciousness of my limitations, my weaknesses and imperfections. Help me to be kind in thought, gentle in word, generous in deed, so that these fruits of my humility may speak to all men of Thy boundless love and care.

Heavenly Father, I am sustained by Thy love. I do not grovel as a slave before Thee. I am Thy child and I may not depreciate that nature within me which shares Thine own eternity. Yet I humble myself before Thee, O God, as I strive to climb the summits of Thy thoughts and seek to fathom the depths of Thy nature. Reward, I pray Thee, my humility with enlightenment. Raise me up from the darkness into the radiance of Thy presence. AMEN.

Alike Before God

The rich and the poor meet together—
The Lord is the Maker of them all.
The poor man and the oppressor meet together;
The Lord giveth light to the eyes of them both.
Would that all the Lord's people were prophets.
Proverbs 22, 2; 29, 13; Numbers 11, 29.

I call to witness heaven and earth that it matters
not whether it be non-Jew or Jew, man or woman,
bond or free; upon each according to his conduct
shall the divine Spirit rest.
Midrash (Yalkut to Judges, 42).

Favoritism means partiality, and both partiality
and favoritism are synonyms for injustice. Favoritism in the law courts, respecting persons in judgment, is an intolerable evil. In public life, favoritism
is the sister of corruption. In the home, favoritism
means the ill rearing and the disrupting of families.
Scripture portrays a long course of tribulations as
the consequence of Jacob's favoritism for Joseph.

The temptation toward favoritism arises from
the diversity of human powers and endowments.
In the home, some children are more obedient than
others; in school, some are more receptive than
others. In social life, some persons are more beautiful and graceful than others; in business some

are more capable than others; in the professions some are more talented than others. But the world is vast. There is a niche for everyone. There are conspicuous places for some; obscure places for others. The bane of favoritism is that it allows no place for "failures" and denies our common childhood to God. The disobedient or unresponsive child, the homely person or the awkward, the incapable or untalented person should not be despised or scorned. A suitable place in human economy should be sought for each and all; and opportunities should be made available so that all may attain their highest possible strength.

Consideration for the poor and lowly is of the very essence of Jewish moral doctrine. The poor and lowly can not fill the roles of the gifted and capable; yet they should not be despised. They should not be "cast as rubbish to the wind." The humanity of every human being no matter how unpromising, should be honored. We should hold fast the faith that he who is unsuited to one task in life may be ideally suited to another. God finds a place for us all. We must emulate His lovingkindness and justice.

Eternal One, Thou art the Father of all. Rich and poor, high and low, gifted and commonplace, are alike precious in Thine eyes. Each has his place, each his work in the world. Bless Thy children with the ability to find each his best place. Grant us the joy of doing the work and fulfilling the tasks for which we are suited. Grant that, beneath all human inequalities, we may discern and ever keep in sight the equality of value which every soul hath before Thee. For "Thou art our Father; we are Thy children. Thou art our Shepherd; we are Thy flock, Thou art our king; we are Thy people. Thou art our possession; we are Thy portion." AMEN.

Cooperation

Two are better than one, because they have a good reward for their labor.

Strengthen ye the weak hands, and make firm the tottering knees.

Ecclesiastes 4, 9; Isaiah 35, 3.

Provide thyself with a teacher and acquire a comrade, and weigh all men in the scale of merit.

Ethics of the Fathers, I, 7.

It is impossible for man to stand alone. He must be near to his fellow-men. One should never say: 'What have I to do with so-and-so; he is not worthy of being my friend; he has sinned; he is wicked.' Nay, man should strive to bring others near unto himself and not repel them.

Judah Loew ben Bezalel, 16th Century (Commentary Path of Life, ad loc.).

Cooperation and concord are the basis of the social order. We live together and are dependent upon one another. Each must give generously to the rest and receive kindness in turn. 'Two are better than one.' Should two contend, both will suffer. Social well-being never comes from conflict, but from cooperation. Working apart is wasteful, working against each other is worse.

Social competitions, social antagonisms, social conflicts mean social upheaval and havoc.

But it is not due merely to worldly wisdom that Judaism asserts: 'Let there be no strife between us,' but because of the larger principle: 'We are brothers.' In God, all men unite; for He is the universal Father. Just as, when we approach God, strife and bitterness cease and we come closer to our brethren, so too when we seek to understand the heart of our brethren, narrowness and selfishness vanish, and we may come nearer to God. Our generosity to our fellowmen and their forbearance toward us, teach us the meaning of God's lovingkindness. Our efforts to bring about unity among men clarify our vision and give fuller meaning to our words when we proclaim: 'The Lord our God is One.' As faith in God leads men to peace, so peace and concord lead men to God.

Lord, Thou art our Father, and we are Thy children. In Thy sight all man-made distinctions vanish, the wise and the simple, the successful and the unfortunate all partake of Thy paternal beneficence. The abundance of Thy lovingkindness shames our selfishness, and the endlessness of Thy mercy rebukes our grudges and hatred. Our fraternal strife is a denial of Thy Fatherhood.

Teach us, O Father, to live in concord with our fellow-men, and thus to prove that we, Thy children, are united in Thee. Thou dost bid us labor in Thy name; teach us to labor in Thy spirit, in patience and in justice. Since Thou hast told us that we are brethren, teach us also how good it is to dwell together in unity. The task which Thou hast set us, to rebuild the world according to Thy plan, is too great for each of us alone, but unite Thou our efforts and we can achieve it. The wind and the rain, the sun and the stars work together harmoniously fulfilling Thy changeless law. O grant unto Thy mortal servants a measure of Thy patience and forbearance, that all of us, parents and children, toilers and planners, races and nations, blend the voices of our hearts to praise Thy name together; so that, when we silence the shoutings of discord and quiet the murmurings of envy, Thy still voice may be heard speaking through the voice of humanity. Amen.

Man's Place in Nature

When I behold Thy heavens, the work of Thy fingers, the moon and the stars which Thou hast established;

What is man that Thou art mindful of him and the son of man that Thou thinkest of him?

Yet Thou hast made him but little lower than the angels and hast crowned him with glory and honor.

Thou hast made him to have dominion over the works of Thy hands; Thou hast put all things under his feet.

Psalm 8.

The first path of humility is to know of God's lovingkindness to all His creatures; and to be conscious of the superiority which He gave to man over all other living beings, as the Psalm says: Thou didst give him dominion over the works of Thy hand. When he will contrast his own little mastery of nature with the exalted power and endless wisdom of God, he will surely be lowly and humble.

Bachya, "Duties of the Heart" (Adapted, Gate of Humility, VI).

Of all the ways of awakening inner reverence in man, the best is the contemplation of the works of God. Their transcendent greatness must inspire awe.

Elijah de Vidas, 16th Century (Beginning of Wisdom I, 2).

In the drama of nature man plays a double role; a servant in lowliness and a king in pride. The magnificence of the heavens shame him into littleness, yet brute creation bows before his prowess. Compared to the eternity of the stars, his life is but a breath; compared to the seasonal withering of plants, his mighty rock-built cities take on an aspect of eternity. Man is but a mote in the sunbeam, and yet is himself a radiant source of light. To the heavens a mortal, to the animals a god.

Both the mighty universe above him, and humble nature below him, speak unto his heart. He must hearken to both voices. From the eternal stars, let him learn patience and reverence for God's greatness. From the world beneath his feet, let him learn kindness and love and how to walk in the footsteps of the Creator. Let him grow to be humble yet confident in his labor; expecting mercy and dispensing kindness; praying for abundance and being himself unselfish. As a humble servant in God's great palace let him be reverent. As a strong worker in God's own workshop, let him continue the works of creation, benevolently, mercifully and unselfishly.

Lord of all worlds, who inhabitest eternity, Thou showest us Thy mercy. We cannot fathom Thy purposes. Thou hast placed us in a wondrous universe, we know not why. Thou art with the contrite and the weak. We trust in Thee and work in Thy name. Thou takest us away as with a flood; we know not whither. We commend our spirits into Thy hand and await eternity.

We call upon Thy name, O Father; give us of Thy strength, that the splendors of the world may not crush us. Grant us of Thy goodness, that our mastery may not corrupt us. Teach us how to revere Thy greatness, and unto those who revere us, how to stand unafraid amidst all of Thy wonders, and, learning from Thy tenderness, how to be gentle to all of Thy creatures. May the heavens declare unto us Thy glory, and may our humble living exemplify Thy lovingkindness. AMEN.

A Prayer of Re-dedication

O Thou Eternal One who hast guided us so long upon the way, we thank Thee for all the blessings with which Thou hast blessed us. We pray that we may be worthy of the faith of our fathers and find in it the strength and comfort which helped them meet the trials and hardships of their lives.

They knew the darkness of oppression and the fear of the unknown but in Thy light they saw light and built a highway in the wilderness. As they built wisely and well for the needs of their time, may we build for the needs of ours so that our children will praise all the work of our hands.

May we never forget that if we build without Thee, we build on shifting sand. Thou who art the confidence of all the ends of the earth, make firm our hearts that in the midst of hate and despair we may declare the glory of Thy ways and restore faith in Thy promise of just and brotherly humanity on a good earth. AMEN.

Repentance

How easy to blame on human nature our personal failure to measure up to the standards we set for ourselves. How easy to excuse, to justify or simplify to say we are sorry and consider the matter closed. The discipline of our faith bids us to keep forever working at self-improvement. It accepts neither the fatalism of those who believe that the environment determines everything nor the fatalism of those who claim that early childhood experiences mould the personality in an iron cast. Judaism teaches that personality is fluid, that it can be changed not only by new situations and new stimuli but even more by inner resolution growing out of new insight and understanding. This insight often comes to one who considers his way of life in the light of God's countenance, that is, in the light of those values and directives which generations of men have held so sacred as to be of God. Our prophets often pleaded with our fathers to seek God and live; to return from their compromises and backslidings and know the mature happiness and profound satisfaction of loyalty to His commandments. May their pleas find a willing response in our hearts. AMEN.

Lead Us, Lord

O lead the hands that grope in darkness,
Take the heart that yearns for Thee!
Take, we pray Thee, take the soul
That fain would find Thee
And in triumph follow Thee.

Thou alone shalt be our master
And Thy word shall be our Law
Lead us, Lord, and we shall serve Thee,
Thee alone for evermore.

Night Prayer

Tremble and sin not, commune with your own hearts upon your beds and be still.

Except the Lord keep the city, the watchman waketh but in vain.

He giveth unto His beloved in sleep.

Into Thy hand I commit my spirit. Thou hast redeemed me, O Lord, Thou God of Truth.

I lay me down and I sleep. I awake for the Lord sustaineth me.

Psalms 4, 5; 127, 2; 30, 6; 31, 6; 3, 6.

> He is the living God to save
> My Rock while sorrow's toils endure.
> My banner and my stronghold sure
> The cup of life whene'er I crave.
> I place my soul within His palm,
> Before I sleep and when I wake;
> And though my body I forsake
> Rest in the Lord in fearless calm.
>
> *Adon Olom (Transl. by Israel Zangwill).*

Night has fallen and the noises of the day are stilled. Toil has been laid aside and man retires to rest. Now that the tumult of the day has ceased, he can hear again the still voice of God; and before the mind sinks into sleep, man can find in the serene presence of the Almighty, a precious moment of quiet contemplation.

The close of the day invites our meditations, for now we can judge ourselves calmly. We have labored arduously during the daylight hours. What have we achieved? Have all our strivings brought us nearer to the haven which we sought? There has been much to do, but how small have been our powers! We see clearly that, alone, we are weak. Yet we know that with the right hand of the Lord to help us we can do valiantly. We must trust in Him and pray that He sustain us.

Perhaps at this eventide we are regretfully reviewing a day misspent; energies squandered in trivial occupations; opportunities for usefulness and righteousness ignored and lost. Yet even the disappointments of such a retrospect need not bring despair, for we may find strength in the assurance that tomorrow God will awaken us to new opportunities and new power.

Such should be the communion of our hearts as we turn away from the accomplishments or the regrets of the day, humbly yet bravely, and face without terror the mysteries of the night. We commit our spirits into the care of our Father. When the Lord is with us we have no fear.

Lord of the spirits of all flesh, a thousand years are but as a day in Thy sight. The days of my life are as a fleeting shadow. Yet it is Thy will that I live my brief moment of life in accordance with Thy law, in righteousness and in truth. Thou dost bid us number our days that we may acquire a heart of wisdom. Therefore I lay before Thee the work of the day that has past. Judge Thou the toil of Thy child. All secrets of my heart, all my frustrated strivings after Thee, Thou knowest. Be Thou merciful unto me.

In the sight of men I may be accounted worthy. They may speak of my achievements and assure me of my success. But in Thy presence I am humble. Weak is my strength, uncertain my resolution, and my accomplishments insignificant. Source of all power, sustain me. Renew my strength and purify my heart to serve Thee in truth.

The day that has passed has been full of temptations. I have yielded to numberless distractions, and forgotten Thy law. I have fallen into the petty thralldom of little sins, evasions and indulgences. Deliver me, O Lord. Let the night's rest restore me. Into Thy hand I commit my spirit, and trust in Thee. Thou wilt redeem me, O God of Truth. AMEN.